CREDIT AND COLLECTIONS

THE SMALL BUSINESS PROFITS PROGRAM

David M. Brownstone
General Editor

Credit and Collections
JOHN W. SEDER

Efficient Accounting and Record-Keeping
DENNIS M. DOYLE

Financing Your Business
EGON W. LOFFEL

How to Run a Successful Florist and Plant Store
BRAM CAVIN

How to Run a Successful Restaurant
WILLIAM L. SIEGEL

Protecting Your Business
EGON W. LOFFEL

Tax-Planning Opportunities
GERALD F. RICHARDS

Forthcoming

How to Advertise and Promote Your Small Business
GONNIE SIEGEL

How to Run a Successful Specialty Food Store
DOUGLASS L. BROWNSTONE

People Management for Small Business
WILLIAM L. SIEGEL

Selling Skills for Small Business
DAVID M. BROWNSTONE

CREDIT AND COLLECTIONS

John W. Seder

A HUDSON GROUP BOOK

—

DAVID M. BROWNSTONE
General Editor

DAVID McKAY COMPANY, INC.
New York

Library of Congress Cataloging in Publication Data

Seder, John.
   Credit and collections.

   "A Hudson group book."
   Includes index.
   1. Consumer credit. 2. Credit cards. 3. Col-
lecting of accounts. 4. Credit. I. Title.
HF5566.S427   332.7'43   77-23295
ISBN 0-679-50735-3

DESIGNED BY JACQUES CHAZAUD

10 9 8 7 6 5 4 3 2 1

MANUFACTURED IN THE UNITED STATES OF AMERICA

52147

78 - 12551

CONTENTS

ONE

Introduction to Credit

*What Is Credit? / Credit Is Limited, Personal, Intangible,
Based on Trust / Our Credit Economy*

WHAT IS CREDIT?

M ONEY, THE ECONOMISTS SAY, IS A MEDIUM OF EXCHANGE,
which means that it is something that is used to facil-
itate the trading or delivery of goods and services from one
person to another.

To put it another way, money (other than gold) has little
or no real value. A dollar bill is intrinsically not worth the
paper it is printed on, except that people will accept it. They
will accept it because they know, or believe, that others will
accept it in turn from them.

Credit Is Limited . . .

Credit is not money, but it is *near money*. Money is a medium of exchange of virtually *universal* acceptance, at least in
the country of origin, but credit is a medium of exchange of
limited acceptance. It is not available to everyone. Moreover,
those who have it cannot use it everywhere. They may use it
freely in some places and not at all in others. There are almost
always limits to the amount they can use, and these limits may
be higher in some places than in others.

. . . Personal . . .

Money is impersonal and unchanging. A dollar bill moves
from hand to cash register to bank to another hand without

changing its character in any way. Credit, by contrast, is extremely personal, special, unique to the individual involved at the particular time. And it is changeable, too. When your boss gives you a promotion and a raise, your credit improves. It is better and larger (although it still has finite limits). And if you proceed to run up large bills all over town and fall behind in paying them, your credit will shrink or disappear entirely.

...Intangible ...

The word credit is derived from the Latin *credere*—"to believe." Credit is believability, credibility. The customer makes a promise to pay, and the merchant believes the promise. Because the customer is a credible person and because the promise is believable, the merchant permits him to carry away goods without receiving anything of tangible value in exchange.

But he does receive something of intangible value—the promise to pay. Because of the customer's credit, his believability, that promise has real value, a precisely measurable value. The proof of its value is that the businessman may take that promise and sell it to somebody else, such as a bank or American Express.

...Based on Trust

The businessman who extends credit is expressing his belief in several different things:

- A belief that the customer *intends* to pay for this purchase;
- A belief that the customer is *able* to pay for it;
- A belief that nothing will happen to prevent him from paying between now and the time payment is due;
- A general belief in the character and integrity of the customer.

The first of these is based partly on trust, partly on history. There is no way to establish positively what anyone's intentions are, because intentions are a state of mind. But there are clues to the customer's state of mind and intentions—clues in his manner, his appearance, his life pattern, and, most important in his record. If he works regularly and pays his bills, if he has established credit and uses it regularly, that provides an excellent basis for trust. It demonstrates that he has kept promises in the past. He has built and is using credit and now has grown to depend upon it, and there is good reason to believe that he will not permit his credit and his credit rating to be damaged by failing to pay this particular bill.

The belief that he is able to pay for this purchase is based upon more tangible things—his job, his house, his car, the family he supports, his bank account—all of these provide evidence of his means and his assets. His other borrowings and bills outstanding are evidence of his liabilities, and it is vitally necessary to inquire about these, too, because there are people who drive fancy cars but are six months behind on the payments. If the amount he owes is large in relation to his income and his cash assets, you should be concerned. But bills and borrowings in reasonable and manageable amounts are a good sign, since they demonstrate that other businessmen have extended credit to this individual.

The third belief concerns external circumstances more than the customer himself. Having concluded that the customer has both the intention and the ability to pay, the businessman further must be willing to believe that nothing will happen to prevent him from paying, that there will be no catastrophe, no unusually bad luck, that he won't lose his job or die in a plane crash or have his home destroyed by a tornado.

How can a sensible, cautious businessman justify risking his money on luck, on blind chance? The answer is that the law of averages is overwhelmingly in his favor. Planes do crash and tornadoes do come through town once in a great while, but the chances that this particular customer will die in the next few weeks, before this bill is paid, are so infinitesimal that they can be ignored.

Why is the fourth item on the list? Why should a businessman be concerned about the general character of the customer if he is satisfied about the particulars we have discussed?

During the 1960s a number of the largest banks and finance companies in the United States lost over a hundred million dollars because they were willing to lend without being concerned about the character and integrity of the borrower. In what became known as the salad oil scandal, a small company borrowed money on the security of soybean oil and corn oil stored in large tanks in Bayonne, New Jersey. The borrowed money was used to buy more oil, that oil was pledged to secure more borrowings, and so on. This type of transaction involves something called a warehouse receipt. The warehouse or storage company receives the oil and gives the owner a receipt, certifying that it has possession of a certain quantity of oil, which it is holding for him. In this particular case, the owner of the company had a very spotty record, including at least one indictment, and his assets and business history gave reason to doubt seriously that he could or would repay the huge sums of money he borrowed. The banks and other lenders knew his background, but they were not concerned about his character because he had collateral, evidenced by warehouse receipts, securing every penny he borrowed. *Or so they thought.* It subsequently turned out that he had forged and doctored many of the warehouse receipts—some of the tanks were only half full and some of them were completely empty.

These lenders violated what many businessmen consider to be a cardinal rule: if the guy is a bum, don't do business with him under any circumstances. No matter how attractive the deal he proposes, no matter how much money you will make on it, no matter how much collateral he has, if he is a chiseler, you will regret dealing with him. If he says, "All the bases are covered, what could possibly go wrong?" the answer is that very possibly he will find something you haven't thought of. In the salad oil case the lenders thought they had all the protection they needed, and indeed they had all the conventional bases covered, but this unscrupulous individual found a new and different way to steal.

OUR CREDIT ECONOMY

An occasional spectacular thievery of this kind can be very expensive to creditors; more common are the less dramatic slow-pay and hard-luck cases that produce ordinary credit problems. But much more common still are the people who pay their bills, usually on time. This is the norm, the ordinary expectation. And this fact is of central importance to the functioning of the modern business economy, which is utterly dependent upon credit. American business uses credit so commonly, so routinely, so pervasively, that it could not function without it. Credit has become a habit. It is extended casually, sometimes almost automatically and without conscious thought.

It is almost unheard of for the buyer of a new car to pay the full price in cash. Indeed, he can usually get by with a very small down payment, or none at all, if he is working steadily. (Of course, many car buyers do it another way—they go to the bank first and borrow the money so that they can pay cash for the car.) Even more rare is the home buyer or condominium buyer who pays cash. The seller does not want to provide credit himself, and as a result it is generally made available by a savings bank or savings-and-loan association; these institutions have a massive pool of capital available for mortgage lending, and they constitute a major industry. In the better stores, and now increasingly in discount and variety stores, in restaurants, at airline ticket counters, and at car rental counters, credit is more and more the rule and cash increasingly the exception. It is probably a fair guess—there are no reliable statistics— that over half of all retail sales are on credit. And the percentage would be considerably higher if we included those transactions in which the merchant accepts a check, and also those in which the customer asks the store to cash his check first before he buys, as is so common in supermarkets and liquor stores. At the producer and manufacturer level and in wholesale trade the proportion of sales on credit is very high, probably over 90 percent. Every manufacturing and distribution company of any size has a credit man, or a whole department, whose sole function is to examine the credit of customers who have ordered goods before the goods are shipped.

In the extension of credit, as in so many things, the United States leads the way, but other developed industrial countries are not far behind us.

All of us as individuals routinely extend credit, too. An employee works for two weeks or a month in the belief that his employer will pay him at the end of that time. We commonly think of a bank as an institution that extends credit to borrowers, but it also works the other way. The depositor puts money in the bank because he believes the bank will return it to him when he wants it; he is extending credit to the bank.'

Over a hundred million people receive credit from electric and gas utilities. With the telephone company the credit runs both ways. The customer pays his regular monthly charge *in advance*;* thus he is extending credit, or belief that the telephone company will provide service for thirty days. On the other hand, the company permits him to make long-distance calls and accumulate message-unit charges in the belief that he will pay for them at the end of the month.

If everyone suddenly stopped extending credit, the economy of this country would experience an immediate and total collapse. Factories would close, there would be a run on every bank, stores would go bankrupt, and it is quite likely that half of the labor force would be out of work within 30 days. We would revert to a primitive economy of barter, an economic stone age.

Thus we see that millions of businessmen regularly deliver goods and services in exchange for a promise to pay later. They are hardheaded and practical people, they are in business to make money, not to give charity or to do favors, and yet they commonly and routinely express trust and belief in matters involving large sums of money.

The next chapter will tell you why they do it.

---

* Most people don't realize this, and the phrasing of the bill is carefully contrived to confuse the issue. When a telephone is installed, the customer is billed *immediately* for the monthly charge; thus, each monthly charge is for the month just beginning, not for the month just ended.

The Advantages of Extending Credit

Two Extreme Viewpoints on Credit / Relations Between Credit and Amount Spent / Collection Problems with the Wealthy / Psychology of Credit and Bill-Paying / The Advantages of Credit / Should You Offer Credit? / Summary

No personal checks accepted. Cash or certified checks only. All work must be paid in full before your car is released.
—Sign in service department of
automobile dealer

THIS SIGN ILLUSTRATES ONE ATTITUDE TOWARD CREDIT—A fairly extreme attitude but not an uncommon one. This businessman considers credit to be a nuisance and a problem. He wants no part of it.

But this businessman, the manager of the service department, is a very unusual one: *he does not want to increase his business.* The service department doesn't make very much money, perhaps none at all. It produces lots of problems and very little profit. Many of the people who come in for service want it done under the warranty, which is no-profit business at best and loss business if he has trouble collecting from the factory.

So the no-credit no-checks policy is used to *discourage* customers. An automobile dealer makes his money from selling cars, not from repairing them. The selling is what interests him; it is the part of the business that gets his attention; it is the reason he went into business in the first place. In the showroom and the selling process he uses credit liberally—rare indeed is the customer who pays cash for a new car, although it is somewhat more common in the case of used cars, particularly older ones.

The dealer is really excited by that showroom. If he had his druthers, he would close down his service department and concentrate all his attention on selling cars. But the manufacturer won't let him do that. He is required as a condition of his franchise to maintain a service department.

This dealer does everything he can to discourage customers from bringing in their cars for service. His employees are rude and abrupt, they require appointments, sometimes days in advance, they show little interest in giving estimates. And, of course, they don't advertise.

TWO EXTREME VIEWPOINTS ON CREDIT

This illustrates the dilemma of credit. If you want to discourage business, don't offer any kind of credit whatever. But the converse of that proposition is that if you want to increase your business, you will probably have to make credit available to your customers in one way or another.

One point of view—let us call it the optimistic approach—is that you should offer credit, selectively and carefully, as a means of expanding your sales and your profits, that you should use credit enthusiastically and aggressively as one of the marketing tools to build your business.

The pessimistic point of view is that you should not extend credit at all if you can avoid it, but that you may have to because your competition does. The credit pessimists feel that extending credit is like putting locks and burglar alarms on your premises or like staying open on Sunday. It does nothing for you, you wish you didn't have to do it because it only brings you additional expense, but it is a fact of life and you have to do it.

The answer probably lies somewhere between these two extremes. Some businesses can get along well without giving credit; others find it an absolute necessity. Some find that the selective and sensible use of credit is very helpful in building business and increasing profits. Others use it reluctantly and grudgingly but find that they have to offer credit in order to maintain their business. If they didn't offer it they would lose sales and their profits would disappear.

RELATION BETWEEN CREDIT AND AMOUNT SPENT

There is generally a direct relationship between the amount your customer spends and the need to offer him credit. The smaller the sale, the more likely it is that it will be in cash; the larger the sale, the more likely that it will involve credit. If you sell one newspaper for 15 cents, you expect a nickel and a dime. But if you deliver the newspaper every day, your delivery boy will go from door to door to collect once a week. If your customer picks it up at your store regularly every day, you will probably collect from him at the end of the month.

A high-style dress shop will usually extend credit liberally to its customers who buy $200 dresses and $75 shoes. The shop will also occasionally sell a $3.50 kerchief on credit, but this is done only as an accommodation to the customer who buys the expensive items.

Some of the costs of a credit transaction are fixed—that is, it costs a certain amount to process a credit sale whether it is $5 or $500. If you extend credit on a sale of only a few dollars, the cost or credit (including losses) will almost certainly wipe out your profit, unless you raise your prices enough to cover it.

The cash customer spends less, the credit customer spends more. Therefore, say the pro-credit forces, offer your customer credit in order to get him or her to spend more. Suppose that a customer comes into your store because she wants to try on the blouse in the window. She saw the price tag and is carrying enough cash to pay for it. Thus she is thinking about spending only within the limits of that cash in her purse. She has an attitude, a mental set, of limitation, of restricted shopping plans.

When you extend credit, you remove the ceiling. Now she is limited only by her clothing budget in general or by her judgment, both of which are more flexible than the amount of cash she has with her. After she tries on the blouse that brought her through your front door, you may suggest that she look at others, some of which carry higher price tags. Then, when she picks the blouse she wants, you are in a position to suggest a skirt that matches beautifully . . . a pair of shoes . . . a purse . . .

Credit, then, is a means to induce your customers to buy more. It also may induce them to "trade up." With the spending ceiling removed by credit, there is a chance that they will choose the more expensive item over the less expensive one, a good chance that they will buy the item they *really* like rather than compromising in order to save money. And maybe they will buy two items instead of one or six instead of two. "You want a six-pack? Have you got your car? Why not take a case?"

People at the lower end of the economic scale would like credit, but they consider it a piece of good luck if it is offered and they are not surprised if it is refused. But the wealthy demand credit and take it for granted that it will be extended. Sometimes they become extremely indignant if it is refused. Some wealthy people assume that they will be granted credit for everything, even smaller purchases, and they carry little or no cash. In smaller towns, where people know each other, they don't even have to carry credit cards. They are known, and therefore their credit is automatic. Similarly, in New York, Jacqueline Kennedy Onassis does not have to carry credit cards —she gets credit with her face. It follows, then, that by offering credit you will attract wealthier people to do business with you, and if you do not offer credit you may be driving away the very class of people whose business would be most profitable.

COLLECTION PROBLEMS WITH THE WEALTHY

Wealthy people get credit easily, often automatically, but that doesn't mean that there are no problems with their credit. On the contrary, there may be major problems. They are sometimes very casual about spending and buying and may not remember what they have spent or what they owe. Since there is no question about their ability to pay, some of them are very relaxed about *when* they pay, and they can become very irritated by even the gentlest of reminders about a bill that is months over-due. In times past, some prominent people made it a practice to pay all of their bills once a year—a practice that did not endear them to their vendors and creditors, particularly those who had the misfortune to sell them something just after their annual payment date.

PSYCHOLOGY OF CREDIT AND BILL-PAYING

Other people who live on credit also make a practice of concentrating the pain and thus in a way minimizing it, or in any case minimizing the time they must endure it. They let bills accumulate and keep postponing the pain; then once a month they pay them all. A few hours of agony and 29½ days of procrastination and pleasure. It may not be a logical approach, but it is a very human one.

Acquiring things is pleasant, paying for them is painful. When you offer credit it seems as though you are offering the pleasure without the pain. You aren't, of course. In reality, you are offering the pleasure now and permitting the pain to be postponed. Human nature being what it is, this is a very attractive offer. Pain later hurts less than pain now—or at least it seems that way. So you have made your customer feel good. And when you make him feel good, you hope that he will be grateful, that he will respond by feeling good will toward you and will express it by doing more business with you.

You also make him feel good in another way. The extension of credit is a form of flattery, a form of ego-building. When you give credit to your customer, you are saying, "I believe in you, I trust you, I have faith that you will pay." You are also saying, "I know that you are rich enough to pay for this purchase. I believe your income and assets are sufficient for you to be able to pay." It is almost like saying, "You are well known, you are somebody, you are a big shot."

A smile and a friendly greeting implies, "I am glad to see you, I like you, you are a nice person." And when your store extends credit, your store becomes a friendly and pleasant place to visit, a place your customers like to come to and will come back to.

When your store demands cash and refuses credit, the message is a very different one. It now carries implications of suspicion, of unfriendliness, disbelief, mistrust. When you demand cash, you are implicitly saying, "I know what a dollar bill is, but I don't know who you are. I don't trust you."

The essence of salesmanship is friendliness and the promise of pleasure. A good salesman hints that you will be happy doing business with him. A good advertisement suggests that you will enjoy buying this product. By flattery and by expressing trust, by offering immediate pleasure and postponed pain, you make it possible for your customer to enjoy doing business with you.

THE ADVANTAGES OF CREDIT

The credit customer will probably buy more and thus increase your volume of business. But it is still entirely reasonable and proper for you to charge higher prices when you sell on credit. It costs you money to extend credit, and it is fair to pass that added cost along to the credit customer. And it should be possible to do so, since the credit customer is less disposed to argue about price.

Credit may help you to reduce costs by smoothing out the fluctuations in your business. Cash buyers usually live from payday to payday. If your customers are paid every Friday, for example, they will spend heavily on Friday and Saturday but your store will be empty from Monday through Thursday. If you have enough staff to handle the end-of-the-week rush, you will be paying people to stand around and do nothing at the beginning of the week. If you don't do that you will be shorthanded when the rush comes, and some people will become impatient and walk out without buying.

Another factor that is becoming increasingly important in this troubled world is that cash attracts robbers. If you do most of your business on credit, you will keep very little cash on your premises, and as this becomes generally known you will be a less attractive target for robbers. When they asked Willie Sutton why he robbed banks, he said, "Because that's where the money is." The fear of robbery and the experience of robbery is one of the central facts in the life of every small businessman today.

If you extend credit and handle it yourself, it should be easier to deal with exchanges and adjustments. If the item is returned, you simply credit the account rather than having to return cash. This is a double-edged sword, however, since the ease of handling the exchange may encourage the customer to return the item; if he paid cash for it he knows that it will be a hassle to get you to give him his money back, and he may decide not to bother.

SHOULD YOU OFFER CREDIT?

There is no easy answer. Moreover, there is no formula for determining the answer. It depends on the type of business you are in, the kind of people you do business with, and many other factors, both rational and irrational. Any generalization or pattern or rule of thumb seems to have a number of exceptions.

For example, consider the grocery business. Fifty years ago the typical grocery store was small. The proprietor knew most of his customers well, waited on them personally, and extended credit liberally. The cost of this attention and credit was built into his prices. Then came the supermarkets, which offered lower prices by cutting out free delivery and credit and by making the customer pick items off the shelves himself and wheel his cart to the cash register himself. Now the two types of store exist side by side. Some people like personalized service, longer store hours, delivery, and credit and they are willing to pay higher prices for those extras. Or in many cases they are constantly running out of money and have no choice but to shop regularly where they can get credit.

As a general rule, it seems reasonable that credit should be extended only to people who are steadily employed and thus have a probable ability to pay. It makes no sense to extend credit to the unemployed and to welfare recipients. And yet it is done all the time. The small grocery store in poor neighborhoods extends credit routinely to welfare mothers "until the next check comes." Not a sound business practice, but a very common one. The losses are high and prices must be set higher to cover these losses.

In a neighborhood where credit makes no sense, where supermarkets with their lower prices are most needed because poor people need to count their pennies, the supermarkets have generally disappeared. They fell victim to robbery, vandalism, and shoplifting but also to the effective competition of the small store, which charges higher prices and offers credit that people living on welfare must have.

The general rule is that credit is far more appropriate for people of means than for the poor. But some of the finest restaurants—the palaces of haute cuisine where dinner for two with wine can cost $100—refuse all credit cards and extend personal credit only to a very few favored customers. The Cadillac dealer is as likely as the Chevrolet dealer to refuse credit and checks in his service department.

It would seem to make sense to extend credit more liberally in the purchase of large tangible items that will last a long time—a house, a car, a refrigerator—as opposed to less tangible things that are rapidly used. The car or appliance can be repossessed.

It would also seem to be the height of folly to offer credit to purchasers of recreational pleasures. Yet we are encouraged to "Fly now—pay later" and to take vacations on credit. These trips cannot be reclaimed by the creditor if they are not paid for.

Liquor is usually not available on credit; in fact, most state laws prohibit taverns and liquor stores from offering credit. (Liquor stores commonly cash checks from known customers, however; this is their way of building good will.) Gambling establishments are not enthusiastic about credit, but some will cash checks. Then, too, the casinos in Las Vegas and the Caribbean extend credit in another form, by sponsoring "junkets" in which transportation, hotel room, and meals are free to those who can be expected to gamble heavily.

SUMMARY

In summary, then, we have identified the following possible advantages to you of extending credit to your customers:

- It may encourage your customers to spend more and increase your total sales.
- It may encourage your customers to trade up to more expensive items on which your margin is higher and thus increase your profits by a greater percentage than the sales increase.
- It is a way of expressing friendliness and trust, of making your store a pleasant place to visit, and the customers may respond with good will toward you, expressed in more buying.
- It may make your customers less concerned about price and less inclined to haggle about price.
- It may help you to attract a wealthier class of customers.
- It may help you to smooth out the fluctuations in your business from day to day and month to month and thus reduce costs.
- It makes exchanges and returns easier to handle (although it may also encourage them).
- It may help discourage robberies if it is known that you keep very little cash.

When all is said and done, you may offer credit to your customers for another reason that is more persuasive than all of these combined: you may *have* to offer it. Your competitors may force you to do it, and you may have to extend credit not in the hope of increasing your business but simply to maintain it and to keep it from decreasing. You may have to run just to stand still.

THREE

The Disadvantages of Extending Credit

Most People Pay Their Bills / Good Intentions—but Bad Luck: Your Biggest Credit Problem / Increased Working Capital / Credit Costs Time / Other Credit Costs / Credit Encourages Splurging / You Can Lose Cash Customers / Resentment Toward the Bill / Summary

MOST PEOPLE PAY THEIR BILLS

MOST OF YOUR CUSTOMERS ARE HONEST. IF THEY BUY from you, they intend to pay and expect to pay.

Does that surprise you? It shouldn't. Remember, we said *most*—not all. And to say that they are honest is not to say that they are saints, or that they are totally pure in heart and mind. They are, in fact, imperfect human beings, even as you and I. They have a good deal of decency in their hearts, but also a little bit of larceny. They have both a basic sense of fair play and a sneaking desire to get something for nothing, to put one over on somebody once in a while. Perhaps you.

Their honesty springs not so much from virtue and sterling character as from an understanding that business is a system of continuing relationships of mutual benefit. They realize that nothing is given away. They know that if goods or services are delivered, they must be paid for. They understand that if they fail to pay for this purchase, they will not be able to get credit for the next one and that other unpleasant things will occur.

Thus if you extend credit you are expressing faith and trust in people who understand the consequences of violating your trust. That understanding provides the strongest assurance that your trust is justified and that they will pay you. They expect to live in your town for a while, they expect to do more business with you in the future, and they expect to seek and receive credit from other businessmen as well as you. This essentially is what keeps them honest and is why they pay their bills.

The basic honesty of most people and their intention to pay what they owe is demonstrated in a very interesting way in the small-loan business. One might logically assume that in times of recession when people lose their jobs or their overtime, they might take out small loans to tide them over. One might expect the small-loan business to increase in bad times.

What actually happens is just the opposite. The small-loan business drops off sharply during recessions. People are less likely to borrow during a time of financial difficulty because they are not sure they will be able to repay the loan. (Of course, there are also people who try to borrow but are refused credit because they have lost their jobs.) When times are good and expectations are high, when people feel optimistic about their jobs and their future incomes, they are more likely to borrow money, because they have confidence in their ability to repay. The same is true of the purchase of a new car or a new home. People make these buying decisions according to how much money they expect to have in the future, not how much they have right now. Thus it is clear that they fully intend to repay what they have borrowed. In bad times, when they are worried about their future income, they will be reluctant to borrow or to buy on credit because they are not sure they can pay. The use of credit depends more on expectations than on need.

Occasionally you will run into a credit customer who is a thief, who has no intention whatever of paying you. But if he intends to steal from you, he has probably stolen from others before. There will almost certainly be information, or at least clues, in his record. The man who has been honest and has paid his bills and suddenly turns to a life of crime is very rare indeed. If he happens to choose you as his first victim, you are almost completely defenseless. If he has means and a good record you will be justified in extending credit to him, and almost any businessman would do the same. So if you happen to encounter him just as he is making the change from honest man to thief, there is no way to protect yourself.*

But this should not be a source of concern. The honorable person who suddenly turns crooked, especially after he has established a good credit record for a number of years, is as rare as snow in July. You probably won't see him once in a lifetime. Indeed, the intentional criminal who has a bad record is almost as rare. He isn't your problem.

GOOD INTENTIONS—BUT BAD LUCK: YOUR BIGGEST CREDIT PROBLEM

Your problem will be the credit customer who *intends* to pay, has the *ability* to pay, and is of good character—that is, he satisfies three of the four tests specified in Chapter One. But he cannot or will not pay for very ordinary and human reasons. He lost his job. He is still working but isn't earning overtime pay any more. He doesn't manage money well and simply got in over his head. He was in an automobile accident. His daughter needs braces, and that will be several hundred dollars he hadn't figured on. Good intentions not lived up to and bad luck (the customer's and now yours, too): these are the principal causes of credit losses, not criminal intent.

The obvious disadvantage of extending credit to your customers is that they may not pay you. And make no mistake about it—this will happen to you. It happens to everybody who extends credit. It happens to the Bank of America and Bankers Trust. It happens to Household Finance and Beneficial Finance. It happens to Macy's and Marshall Field. All men are mortal. The road to hell is paved with good intentions. Things

---

* The underworld understands this very well and has learned to take advantage of it in a manner that is very difficult to combat. They secretly buy working control of a business that has a good credit rating and has paid its bills regularly. They order huge quantities of merchandise on credit and then—just as their vendors and creditors are beginning to get suspicious—they file for bankruptcy, having looted the company of all of its assets. The vendors are defenseless against this unless they are alert enough to detect clues of changes in ownership.

don't always go as planned. That is why there are erasers on pencils and that is why there are credit losses.

INCREASED WORKING CAPITAL

The possibility of losses—no, make that the *certainty* of losses—is the major disadvantage of offering credit to your customers. It is the major one, but it is far from being the only one. A second major disadvantage of extending credit is that it will increase your working-capital requirements, the amount of money you have to put into and leave in your business in order to keep it going.* When you extend credit to a customer, it is the same as lending him money. When he buys merchandise he would normally pay you in cash, but instead of giving you the cash, he gives you a promise to pay you cash later. You have exchanged the opportunity to receive a dollar now for the hope of receiving it later. It is a dollar you don't have.

But your cash needs haven't changed at all. Your creditors have not extended the time for you to pay. Your cash on hand has decreased, your cash needs remain the same, and therefore you will have to put an additional dollar of cash into your business. Put an additional dollar in or leave a dollar in that you might otherwise take out—it amounts to the same thing.

If you have been doing business strictly in cash and then you decide to extend credit, and if everything else remains the same, you will need an additional amount of capital in your business equal to the total amount that all of your customers owe you at any given moment. If you plan to extend and carry credit (accounts receivable) totaling $10,000, you will have

---

* For those who may be unfamiliar with the term *working capital*, a bit of definition. The money or capital you need to start and continue your business is of two kinds—money for permanent or fixed assets (buildings, machinery, equipment, freezer cabinets, neon signs) and the money for assets that are constantly moving in and out or turning over (your cash, your inventories of merchandise and work in process, your raw materials and supplies, and your receivables, amounts owed to you by those to whom you have extended credit). These moving assets are called "current assets." The money you owe to *your* creditors—accounts and bills due and payable—these are current liabilities.

If you add up all of your current assets and subtract your current liabilities, the resulting figure is your working capital.

to invest another $10,000 in your business one way or another. It is an additional $10,000 that would not have been required if you had continued to operate on a cash basis.

If you borrow the additional $10,000, you will have to pay interest on it. Another way to borrow is to factor—that is, to sell your accounts receivable to a commercial finance company, with or without recourse. If you do this, the finance company will "discount" your receivables. They will buy them from you but pay you somewhat less than the customer owes. The discount, which will not be a small one, is the equivalent of interest and also compensates them for handling the collections.

Extending credit means that you carry receivables. And you will handle your receivables in much the same way as your inventories. Suppose, for example, that you open a store and stock it with $50,000 worth of goods on the shelves. You will then have $50,000 tied up in inventories all the time—permanently. When you sell an item and it is paid for, you can't put the money in your pocket. If you did that, your shelves would soon be bare and you would be out of business. Generally, every time you sell an item you will reorder another to replace it. And so, although the inventories on your shelves are constantly turning over, you will have to keep that $50,000 permanently committed to inventory. You may put it up in cash, you may borrow it from a bank or from your suppliers, but you have to keep it there.

It works the same way with credit extended to your customers. When one pays you, you don't put the money in your pocket; rather, you will extend a similar amount of credit to another customer. Or perhaps to the same customer for a new purchase. So the total amount of your receivables is a revolving fund. The component parts are constantly changing, but the total remains committed as part of your permanent investment in your business.

If you did not have that money committed to carry receivables, you could use it for other purposes or you might put it in the bank and earn interest. Therefore, the loss of this potential interest is an additional cost of extending credit. This is what economists call "opportunity cost." By having the money tied up in receivables and permanently committed to support your credit program, you are missing other opportunities to use that money to earn money.

CREDIT COSTS TIME

Another major disadvantage of credit is that it costs you time—time that you can ill afford to spare and that you need for many other things. As an entrepreneur and a proprietor, you have long since learned that the forty-hour week does not apply to you. A hundred hours is more like it. You have discovered that running your business takes everything you have, all your energy and attention, and then some. When you are open for business you spend all your time dealing with customers, and then after you close your doors you will stay for long hours to deal with paper work and dozens of details. And when you go home, you find yourself still thinking about the problems of your business. They may keep you awake, or you may find yourself dreaming about them. If so, you have plenty of company, for that is the lot of the entrepreneur.

Extending credit will put additional demands upon your time. You will have to give considerable time and thought to deciding whether to approve credit for this individual or that one. Depending on the nature of your business, the credit decision may be based on a formal procedure, including application forms, credit interviews, credit bureau inquiries, and reference checks. Or, it may be an informal procedure in which you make your decision primarily upon your intuition and your knowledge of the customer and his character. But however you make the decision, you will have to give it some serious attention and thought. You are in for trouble if you don't.

If, after the initial credit decision in the affirmative, the customer turns out to be a problem, you will spend much more time with a number of decisions at various stages. The first question is, What kind of person is he and should you offer him more credit? The next decision is, How much credit should you let him have, how high should you let his bills run up before you call a halt? Now that he owes you money, you will have to try to keep track of him, to keep informed about his good luck and his bad luck, whether he is fired or promoted, and his travel plans. Especially international travel for extended periods. If he falls behind in payments, should you be concerned? How much should you be concerned? At what point should you stop extending credit and demand cash for future purchases (and run the risk that he will take his business elsewhere, where his credit is still good)? If you succeed in maintaining contact with him, he will give you excuses for his failure to pay and new promises to pay. How much of his story and his promises should you believe? At what point do you write him off, or call in a collection agency or a lawyer?

All these decisions are hard ones involving individual judgment. Each case is different; there is no magic formula to provide the answers. You will have to give a great deal of your time and attention to making these decisions, and you will find that they take a lot of emotional energy. Alternatively, you can hire somebody to do this worrying and make these decisions for you; then it will cost you money to pay his salary. You will still have to watch him carefully to make sure he is doing the job right.

It is probably fair to say that most small businessmen devote a major part of their time to dealing with credit problems— deciding whether to extend credit and how much, deciding how to deal with delinquents, dunning them, listening to their excuses and promises. (And, of course, making excuses and promises to their own creditors.)

There are also expenses in connection with making credit decisions at various stages even before credit becomes a problem. If you handle your own credit, it will cost you something just to educate yourself and prepare for it. You may buy one or more books like this one and go to some classes. If you have a credit application form (as you probably should), you will either buy standard forms or prepare your own and have them printed. The laws governing extension and refusal of credit and credit reporting are becoming increasingly complex; you may decide to get and pay for some good legal advice about what you can and cannot do. There is the cost of the time spent by your employees in dealing with credit matters.

OTHER CREDIT COSTS

If you belong to a credit bureau, you will probably pay a yearly membership fee plus a dollar or two for every inquiry you make. If you do your own credit checking, you will have the costs of correspondence and telephoning. One phone call may take only a couple of minutes, but many phone calls can add up. And it multiplies when you get a busy signal or a "He's out this morning; can you call back this afternoon?" The message units mount up, too. If you extend credit through one of the national credit card companies, they will discount your price by several percentage points when they pay you. If your business is big enough to give you negotiating clout with the credit card people, you may be able to get the discount down to 3 percent or possibly even a fraction lower, but most smaller retailers pay as much as 5 or 5½ percent in discounts.

When you get to serious collection problems, you will have another variety of costs: collection letters and telephone calls, the very heavy discounts charged by collection agencies, and lawyer's fees, which can be very sizable in relation to the amount of money involved.

CREDIT ENCOURAGES SPLURGING

In Chapter Two we said that one of the advantages of offering credit is that you encourage your customer to spend more. The cash customer must limit himself to the cash he is carrying, and when you extend credit you remove that limit. Credit helps to increase your business and your profits, but problems may come with it. A fair number of people can be counted on to do something foolish when they are restrained only by their own judgment and self-discipline. By offering credit you may allow or possibly even encourage your customers to lose control, to splurge, to spend beyond their means, to buy things they cannot really afford and will have trouble paying for. There may be increased hassle and ill will in dealing with customers who splurged and lost control of themselves and then had second thoughts when they got home or later when the bill arrived. A big sale followed by a return produces no profit for you and takes time to deal with.

YOU CAN LOSE CASH CUSTOMERS

If you extend credit to some of your customers, you may run the risk of losing others. Intelligent and thoughtful people know that offering credit costs you money, and they assume that you have raised your prices to recoup this cost. Therefore they may feel that if they pay cash they are paying a higher price for a service they do not care to use. Some people will not think about this, or if they do think about it they will assume that the amounts involved are too small to be concerned about. Others will haggle with you about the price or ask for a discount for paying cash. But your real concern is the customer you will never know about and never see, the one who avoids you because you offer credit. This is the individual who makes it a definite policy to deal only with cash-and-carry or discount stores because he firmly believes that he always gets better value by buying from stores that don't give credit.

RESENTMENT TOWARD THE BILL

Finally, there is another disadvantage to credit which is difficult to measure, difficult to pin down, less tangible but no less real. We said earlier that offering credit is an expression of friendliness, of flattery and ego-building, and we also said that buying on credit involves immediate realization of pleasure combined with postponement of pain. But things have a way of balancing and evening themselves out. The friendliness in offering credit is offset later by your bill, which is a distinctly unfriendly communication. No matter that the money is owed, no matter that you have a right to expect payment, it is just not possible to come across as pleasant and friendly when you ask for money. And so, just as the original friendliness may have produced good will, the billing may arouse resentment. Not logical, but very human. All of us feel a certain resentment toward our creditors because they have a measure of power over us. And the more trouble we have paying, the more power they seem to have, and the more we resent them for it. Nobody loves a bill collector.

Consciously or subconsciously your customer may resent you, his creditor. And he may express this resentment by avoiding you. He may stay away from your store and go down the street instead.

SUMMARY

We have identified a number of possible disadvantages of extending credit:

- Losses, when the customer fails to pay.
- Increased working capital required in your business in order to carry customer receivables.
- Opportunity cost—the loss of interest or other income that you could earn if you invested that money somewhere else.
- Interest or financing charges on the additional capital, if you have to borrow it.
- Time and attention required to deal with a variety of credit decisions and problems.
- The additional expense of credit checking, credit bureau memberships and fees, discounts on credit card sales and costs of collection agencies and lawyers.
- Credit may encourage your customers to splurge and then have trouble paying.
- They may be more likely to return the item or demand adjustments if they have not paid for it yet.
- Extending credit may cause you to lose cash customers.
- Your customers may resent you because they owe you money and may avoid you as a result.

FOUR

Should You Extend Credit
to *This* Customer?

*The Five C's of Credit / Character / Capital / Collateral /
Capacity / Conditions / Mathematical Rating Formulas /
How to Judge the Credit-Worthy Character / Taking
Credit Seriously*

WE HAVE SEEN THAT CREDIT IS BELIEF AND TRUST, AND we have seen—somewhat to our surprise—that the entire American business system seems to run on trust and would come to a halt without it. The massive extension of credit is essential to keep the economic wheels turning. While it is encouraging to know that most people are honorable and pay their bills, that generalization does not help you in making your basic credit decisions. When you are trying to make a decision about one customer in particular, it is of very little value to you to know that 97 or 98 percent of all bills are paid in full and on time. Trust is all very nice, but you must approach each credit decision with *mistrust*, with suspicion, with skepticism.

Obviously an overt expression of suspicion will antagonize the customer and may damage the future relationship or perhaps even cause the loss of the present sale, and so you will show your suspicion as little as possible. But you feel it and are guided by it. And try as you may to be gentle and polite in your questioning, it is bound to come through to some extent. Nobody likes to have to probe, to question, to be suspicious. And nobody likes to be questioned, to be doubted. An atmosphere of questioning and suspicion is destructive of the kind of friendly and cordial business relationship you want to establish with all your customers.

Naturally, if it is a new customer, you hope he will do a lot of business with you in the future, and you regret the necessity of irritating him by close questioning about his credit standing and his ability to pay. Yet you must do it, as gently and politely as possible. There is no escaping it. And indeed, if he is the honorable and trustworthy individual that you think and hope he is, he will not have any serious objection to establishing and demonstrating his reputation and his background. He understands that you are entitled to know his credibility before you extend him credit.

In making your basic decision to grant or withhold credit you must first determine whether you are dealing with criminal intent, with someone who has no intention of paying, an out-and-out liar and thief. There are such characters abroad in the land, and they never cease trying their confidence games on honest merchants.

You will look with great suspicion upon the complete stranger with no known roots in the community, no identifiable (or believable) place of residence or employment, no bank reference or Social Security number. Or the individual with no documents of any kind—no driver's license, no credit card, not even a library card—and an elaborate story to explain why he has none. He may tell you that he was just discharged from the service, he just came to this country to visit relatives, or he was mugged and his wallet was stolen. You will come to be amazed at the ingenuity and imagination which is used in concocting hard-luck stories, replete with details of names and places and employers that you have never heard of and cannot possibly check.

The individual who approaches you with malice aforethought, with criminal intent, is likely to be so obvious and so lacking in subtlety that you will lose little time in making a decision. In all probability you will not only refuse him credit but do everything you can to get him out of your place of business as soon as possible. You will identify him by the absence of any of the indicia of a stable life pattern, by his total lack of credible or checkable facts and details. If he has a settled and honorable pattern of life and behavior, there will be certain verifiable facts about him. If not, you will probably be able to tell pretty fast.

So, as we have said, the out-and-out criminal is not your major credit problem. The problem is the honorable people with good intentions who fail to keep their promises. The credit customer who becomes a collection problem is almost never a thief or a basically malevolent or immoral person. Rather, he is an ordinary mortal, full of all of the imperfections that characterize the breed. When he bought the merchandise he undoubtedly meant to pay for it, and even after several months he still intends to pay—if and when he can. His failure to pay does not stem from evil intent but rather from procrastination, bad luck, poor planning, poor budgeting, impulsive buying beyond his means (and this may include the item he bought from you and owes you for), unrealistic intentions and hopes, inability to control the spending of other members of his family, poor memory, not wanting to think about unpleasant things—and a host of other accidents that happen to and weaknesses that are commonly found in members of the human race. Your basic credit decision involves an individual with good and sincere intentions. But how can you be sure . . . ?

The answer is that you cannot be absolutely certain about this, any more than you can about any other aspect of your business, or life itself. So you must try to establish what the probabilities are. You must learn enough about the customer to make a determination as to whether there is a very strong probability that he will pay. You want the odds as strongly as possible in your favor.

THE FIVE C's OF CREDIT

Textbooks and treatises on credit commonly refer to the five C's of credit:

Character

The great financier J. Pierpont Morgan was once asked at a Congressional hearing how he decided whether to lend money to a businessman. He answered, "Character, sir, character—nothing else matters." His point was that in an imperfect world integrity and ability provide the best assurances that it is possible to get. The able and honorable man will pay, will find some way to pay despite whatever difficulties he may encounter. Indeed, he may spend the rest of his life trying to pay what he owes. Morgan's opinion was perhaps somewhat overstated for dramatic effect, but it is a valid point of view that deserves respect.

Capital, or Net Worth

How much does he have in the form of net assets after deducting liabilities? How much is he worth? If he sold everything and paid all his bills, how much would he have left? The capital, or net worth, test is very appropriate for most business borrowers, but it is not very useful to a retailer who deals with individual customers. For one thing, it is usually very difficult to get reliable information on the net worth of an individual; he and his bank are probably the only ones who know, and they will probably not tell. Furthermore, it is quite common to find people even in the middle- and upper-income brackets who have very little net worth, sometimes practically none if you exclude their life insurance. They earn a good deal of money and spend all of it.

Collateral

What assets does he have that can be pledged to secure repayment of what is owed, assets that can be seized and sold if he does not pay? Again, this is more appropriate for a business credit situation, although it does apply to individuals who are buying homes and automobiles and would apply in certain other areas, such as home improvements.

Capacity, or Ability, to Repay

This is a broader and much more important test than capital or collateral. Capacity is a measure not only of assets but of past earnings and future earning power, the stability and continuity of the individual's job, the value of his home and other assets, if any, his outside income and the incomes of his wife and other members of his family—in other words, a total measure of his assets and income, past, present, and potential. The total is balanced against his liabilities and obligations to his dependents, the holder of his mortgage, and his other creditors.

Capacity also involves other considerations, such as his age, health, smoking habits, and recreational activities. Dangerous hobbies are a minus. A quiet and settled life pattern is a plus. Illegal drugs or excessive drinking is a minus. And so on. Remember that the fundamental question is the *probability* of repayment, and any information is relevant if it tells something about the individual and his life style that may affect his capacity to repay and the probability that he will repay.

Economic Conditions

Unlike the other four criteria, all of which relate solely to the individual himself, this involves consideration of factors external to him. Is there a possibility that economic developments beyond his control may affect his capacity to repay? He may be a person of fine character, with a good job, money in the bank, and a life style that demonstrates honor, integrity, and responsibility. But all of this may mean nothing if his employer's business is going badly, or if the economy of the area is heavily dependent upon crops that are damaged by drought. Or if the general economy collapses into a severe depression. During the 1930s, millions of honorable people and businesses failed to pay their bills, despite the best of character and intentions and what had appeared to be sufficient capacity to pay. The problem was caused by unforeseen economic conditions beyond their control.

Character, capital, collateral, capacity, and economic conditions—these are, according to the textbooks, the five criteria you should consider in determining whether to grant credit. Unfortunately, like many things in textbooks, they are somewhat limited in practical value to you as a businessman who has to make a decision.

Character is important, nobody will argue about that. But

how do you determine what a person's character is? How much do we really know about other people, even our close friends? You may think you know a good deal about a person and his behavior when things are going well, but how will he react to adversity? You and other creditors may know him to be a successful, prosperous, well-ordered person, but you may not know all sides of his personality. He may not have the strength to deal with misfortune, he may go to pieces if things go against him.

In the last analysis, it comes down to common sense and judgment, and nobody has yet figured out a set of rules or a formula for exercising good judgment and using common sense. You will sometimes have a sixth sense, a feeling or intuition that you cannot explain precisely or logically. You may feel that somehow something just doesn't ring true or feel right about a certain individual, even though his record and his references seem to be excellent. In other cases the record may be poor, but your intuition tells you to take a chance because there is something about that person that makes you feel confident and comfortable.

It probably makes good sense to pay attention to your feelings and your intuitions, unless you have found from past experience that they are unreliable. Be sensible and flexible about it, though, and go very carefully about letting a comfortable *feeling* override a lot of negative *information*. Virtually all important decisions are products of a number of considerations, facts and opinions, some of which cannot be precisely measured and some of which are not even consciously recognized. Don't forget that there is a lot of wisdom in your subconscious that expresses itself in those intuitions and feelings that you can't define or explain; this wisdom is valuable and you should not hesitate to let it work for you.

If you make a mistake in granting credit, it can be an expensive mistake. Accordingly, there is something to be said for erring on the side of caution. If you follow the policy, "When in doubt—don't," you should be able to limit your credit losses.

MATHEMATICAL RATING FORMULAS

Some credit analysts suggest the use of mathematical rating formulas. Here is one formula reportedly used by an agency of the federal government:

Character	30%
Attitude toward obligations	15
Ability to pay	15
Prospects for the future	12
Business history	10
Ratio of value of property to income	7
Ratio of monthly mortgage payment (or rent) to monthly income	6
Associates	5
	100%

The theory is that you assign numerical ratings to the individual in each of these categories and then weight them according to the percentages. A passing grade is 51 percent. Or should it be 65 percent? Or 75?

The list of categories is a useful one. All five considerations are important and deserve your attention and analysis. But the percentages assigned are arbitrary, and you may find that the mathematical exercise is not especially helpful. Who is to say that character should be assigned 30 percent rather than 27— or 32? Ability to pay and prospects for the future are almost the same thing, or different facets of the same thing, and it is difficult to treat them separately.

This formula or any other formula provides a useful checklist, but it is misleading in that it appears to provide numerical precision in an imprecise matter. People are constantly searching for absolute certainty in an uncertain world. They keep trying to express judgments in exact numbers, but the exactness is artificial. There is no formula, no arithmetic that you can substitute for using your head and common sense.

HOW TO JUDGE THE CREDIT-WORTHY CHARACTER

The all-inclusive term *character* combines and includes a number of elements that are important to your credit-granting decision. The best credit risk is a solid, stable, responsible person who is conscientious about keeping his commitments and promises, who has a life style that is characterized by responsibility and steadiness—a person who promises no more than he can deliver and who delivers what he promises. A person who is known, who has been around for a while and will be around for a good while longer.

Stability and continuity of employment and residence and indeed of personal habits are very desirable. Beware of those who are constantly moving, constantly changing jobs—and spouses. Beware of those who are always revising their life styles; every time you meet them they are "into" something new. First yoga, then organic foods, then encounter sessions. They may be creative and interesting people to talk to or to party with, but they are probably not very good credit risks. A certain continuity, a certain calmness and steadiness is what you are looking for.

Another way to put it is that your best credit risk is the person who is *in control* of himself and his life. Some people are always in trouble, always in turmoil; their lives seem to be an endless succession of problems, bad decisions, and bad luck. They seem to be at the mercy of events and circumstances. They are constantly buffeted about by fate, and as a result their lives are disorganized and unpredictable. They seem to be off balance most of the time.

Stability, responsibility, predictability, even stodginess and dullness—these are the characteristics of a good credit risk. Flamboyance, uninhibited behavior, excitement, impulsiveness, unpredictability—these are the marks of a poor credit risk. Our society may need more poets and musicians, but it is probably not a good idea to extend credit to them, unless they also have what musicians call a day job.

TAKING CREDIT SERIOUSLY

Credit is a serious business. It involves the risk of your money, and so you take it seriously. It is important that the customer take it seriously, too. Therefore it is essential that the request for credit be discussed and treated seriously as a matter of importance. The discussion should not be mixed with salesmanship or small talk. The atmosphere and your manner during the discussion should make clear to the customer that credit is not a right but a privilege that you may grant or withhold. If credit is granted, it is not to be taken lightly, not to be abused. If the customer feels that credit is a service that he is entitled to automatically, that he can take for granted, he may be very relaxed about paying what he owes. If you discuss it in an offhand way and treat it lightly and casually, he will be casual about it, too.

It is important to start out on the right foot with a credit customer. You must make clear to him that you expect him to pay his bills on schedule, and there should be a clear understanding between you as to what that schedule is. If there are any interest or late charges, you must explain them carefully and make sure he understands. Misunderstandings and confusion about credit terms—or claimed misunderstandings—can come back to haunt you when you are collecting.

There is an old saying, and a good one, in the credit world: "Accounts well opened are half collected."

Some businessmen will not grant credit unless they have received a formal written credit application. It is important to have dates, places, and names of employers and references in your files. But it is also important psychologically. The customer will take a serious attitude toward the obligation if he is required to fill out a formal application.

In a credit application you should try to get all of the following information:

- Name.
- Age.
- Present home address and phone number. How long there? (If less than two years, previous residence address.)

- Monthly mortgage payment or rent.
- Social Security number.
- Place of employment, address, and telephone number.
- How long there? (If less than five years, previous employment going back five years.)
- Job title or type of work.
- Immediate superior.
- Salary. Bonus or commissions, if any.
- Other income, if any.
- Liabilities: what debts to banks, finance companies, auto loans, credit cards, other merchants.
- Number and age of dependents.
- Do you own an automobile? Make and age? How much owing?
- List credit cards and charge accounts.
- Bank accounts, both checking and savings.
- References, business (2).
- References, personal (2).

You will probably want to add some "fine print" at the bottom of the application, so that when the customer signs it it becomes a contract that binds him after credit is granted. For example, you might want to specify that you continue to have a lien or security interest in the goods purchased until they are paid for. You might put in language that the customer authorizes you to investigate his credit and to report on him to credit bureaus. If you charge interest or finance charges, they should be specified in some detail.

It will probably not be possible to get all your customers to give you all the information listed above, but you should get as much as you can. And of course there is no assurance that the answers will be truthful. Most people will tend to answer accurately when they know that the information can be easily checked. On such subjects as other assets, other income, and other liabilities, it may be impossible to verify the information given, and therefore fictitious answers may be more common.

If you are able to get a major part of the information shown above, you will in most cases find a number of useful clues that will aid you in making your basic decision about whether or not to grant credit. The length and stability of employment and residence are of major importance. When the customer has held his present job for only a few months, it is especially important that you insist upon knowing his previous employment history. The kind of company he works for and the kind of work he does will tell you something about him as a person and about the steadiness of his life style.

If he claims a middle-class income and life pattern, you expect to find that he owns an automobile, and it will be grounds for some surprise if he does not—not grounds for refusing credit but merely grounds for surprise. Most middle-income families in this country own cars, and you are entitled to be curious as to why your customer is different.

You will be somewhat concerned if the customer has trouble thinking of references, and you will be more concerned if he gives references but asks you not to call them. You will be surprised if the customer has a stable employment and residence pattern but no charge accounts, and you will be especially surprised if he has neither charge accounts nor credit cards in this day and age. Credit has become so pervasive in our society that almost everybody uses it in one way or another. If a customer will not admit to having any charge accounts or credit cards, you have to suspect that (1) he has them but won't admit it because he is delinquent with his other creditors, (2) he has abused his credit in the past and his charge accounts have been closed and his credit cards revoked, or (3) the other stated facts about his employment, residence, and income may be false. There may be a plausible explanation, but you must ask for it and weigh it very carefully. After all, if he doesn't have credit with anybody else, that tells you something. Why does he suddenly want credit for the first time? You will want to proceed very cautiously with this individual.

Now that you have learned as much as possible from the customer about himself and his background, you must decide whether to believe everything he told you or to verify it independently. In the next chapter we will discuss some of the ways you can check on him.

When all is said and done, it is important to remember that if you extend credit you are virtually certain to have losses. Credit involves risk; the two cannot be separated. The test of a successful credit policy is not to avoid risk—that is impossible—but to hold to an acceptable level of risk.

If you reject all or almost all applications for credit, you are probably being too strict. If you approve almost all of them, you are undoubtedly being too liberal.* That leaves a huge middle ground, and there is no formula to guide you and no expert who can give you any guarantees or assurances. You will have to use common sense and judgment. And if you are like everybody else, you will learn the hard way: from experience.

---

* One of the largest and most spectacular business failures in history was the collapse in 1975 of the W. T. Grant retail chain. Some cynics suggested that Grant used a mirror as a credit application. The customer was asked to hold the mirror in front of his nose and mouth, and if moisture condensed on the mirror, the credit was granted. The story is not true, but it does appear that excessively liberal credit practices, including the granting of credit to people who were turned down everywhere else, was a major factor in the demise of the company.

FIVE

Credit Checking

Most Credit Applications Require Checking / How to Do It Yourself / Credit Bureaus and Reporting Services

L ET US ASSUME NOW THAT YOU HAVE CAREFULLY CONSIDERED the question of whether you will extend credit to your customers and have decided in the affirmative. Now you are beginning to receive requests and applications from your customers for credit, and you have to make some decisions. You will have a few easy decisions and a lot of hard ones.

In some cases the information the customer presents about himself is so sketchy or his record so questionable that the decision makes itself—you know immediately that you must refuse credit to this individual. It is an easy decision, and of course there is no need to check his record or get independent verification (or denial) of what he has told you.

In other cases you know the individual so well or his assets are so large that you can immediately approve credit. This is another easy decision that probably does not require checking. (However, in this case it might not hurt to do some checking. You may be satisfied as to the customer's wealth, but you should also know something about his paying habits. As was mentioned earlier, many wealthy people are notoriously slow payers.)

MOST CREDIT APPLICATIONS REQUIRE CHECKING

The easy decisions don't give you any trouble or take any time, but that leaves the great middle ground, which will include the majority of your credit customers. These are people whose record seems fairly good but not sensationally good, people who give you some confidence but not enough, and also those who give you some doubts but not serious ones. Then there are those whose applications look perfect, but too perfect; they look so good that you have a feeling that something has been falsified or left out. And there are those who give you no reason for concern except that you are *always* concerned because you have been burned in the past. You may have come to the conclusion that you will run checks on all your credit customers, no matter how well you know them or think you know them, as a matter of policy. This is not a bad idea, by the way; if you're going to be in the credit business you might as well be serious about it.

HOW TO DO IT YOURSELF

Now you are ready to do some checking. How do you go about it?

One possibility is to do it yourself. You will start, probably, by getting on the telephone. With a pleasant voice and manner you can usually get a good deal of information on the telephone in a fairly short time. Some people may not be willing to volunteer anything but will give you a confirmation or denial of information that you already have.

Your customer's employer is a good place to start. For one thing, he is extremely important to you—he is paying the salary that is the ultimate source of the money that will be paid to you. Secondly, it is probably not necessary to ask for any additional information. You probably already have most or all of the facts and figures you need; you merely want to verify them, and you are very likely to get a verification in a minute or two on the phone. Basically you want to know whether the customer has told you the truth about the kind of work he does and how long he has held his job. If you tell his boss or the personnel department of his company what he has told you, they will probably be willing to tell you whether it is accurate or not.

Salary is more difficult. If you ask the question you will probably not get an answer. On the other hand, if the customer has told you what his salary is, or if you feel like making a guess, it may be possible to quote a figure and get an answer such as "Yes, that's right," or "That's about right," or "That's in the ball park."

Occasionally you may find an employer who is unusually cordial and volunteers information because he is interested in getting information from you. If, for example, you are a Rolls Royce dealer and your customer has a Ford income, his employer may be interested to know that he is talking to you and he may let you know that the amount of credit you are considering is inappropriate.

In addition to calling the customer's boss or the personnel department, it is sometimes an interesting exercise to place a call to the customer himself. This will tell you whether he is well known to the switchboard operator. Another approach is to ask for "Somebody in the Such-and-such Department" or to say "I have been discussing a matter with Mr. So-and-so, but I understand he is out today; can you connect me with somebody who works with him?" You may get a secretary or a co-worker on the phone who will tell you about his work and how long he has been there. If you are playing one of these games and Mr. Customer himself answers the phone, the best move is to hang up.

Every name on the credit application is a reference that may be checked, although some will give more information than others and some will give none at all. Try his landlord, try other merchants. Any information you can get will help to fill out the picture.

Another thing. *Be sure to check his personal and business references.* That seems fairly obvious, and yet many creditors fail to do it. They don't want to take the time, and they often assume that any reference the customer gives has been carefully selected to give nothing but praise. This is not necessarily so. Some people have a hard time thinking of anybody who will speak completely enthusiastically about them, and in the absence of strong references they have to give you lukewarm ones. Some people give references without telling the reference that they are going to do so, and the reference may be irritated by this and may speak more frankly than you might expect. The reference may not want to give you critical comments on the phone, but if he is cool or unenthusiastic, that tells you something. And if he seems not to know the person very well or to have trouble remembering who he is, that will tell you that you should proceed with caution.

The best source of information other than the employer is also one that is least likely to tell you anything useful on the phone—the customer's bank. He is the bank's customer, too, and they owe their first loyalty to him rather than to you. Most bankers will be suspicious of your identity if you call on the phone and they may even refuse to confirm or deny that the individual has an account there. If you write them a letter, enclosing a stamped, self-addressed return envelope, you may do a little better. Even in that case, they may tell you no more than that relations with your customer have been "satisfactory."

The best approach in dealing with a bank is to include in your letter a number of very specific questions, in the hope that they will answer some of the easier ones even if they refuse to answer the more delicate ones. For example:

"We are told that _____ has a regular checking account with you. Can you confirm?"

"Have your relations with him been satisfactory?"

"Has _____ ever allowed his account to be overdrawn?"

"What is the average balance maintained in his account?" (The banker won't give you a number, but he may give you something like medium three figures, which would be $400 to $600, or low four figures, which would be over $1,000.)

"Have you ever extended loans to _____? Is any balance currently outstanding? Has the relationship been satisfactory? Are payments being made on schedule?"

"We are considering extending credit to _____ in the amount of $_____. Would you recommend doing so?"

There is no way to assure that you will get what you want from a banker. Each contact will be different. In some cases you may be surprised by the stone wall you run into, and in other cases you may find that questions are answered and information is volunteered. Most banks have a credit inquiry department and expect to receive inquiries, but they are somewhat more attuned to handling questions about businesses than about individuals.

Banks in smaller towns may be more communicative, especially if you know the banker personally, but this is by no means certain. The customer may know him personally too and perhaps socially, and the banker may be afraid that anything he says will get back.

Keep in mind also that the bank does not know everything. Some people are very careful about maintaining their checking accounts and their loans in a responsible way but make a practice of stalling their other creditors. Your customer may be months past due with merchants all over town, but as long as he doesn't bounce checks the banker may never hear about it.

You may be able to enter into a reciprocal arrangement with a bank in which you provide them with the details of your credit experience with various individuals and they in turn are somewhat more communicative when you make inquiry about one of their customers. This mutual exchange of information is very common and is the source of much of the data in the possession of the credit bureaus and credit reporting services. They trade information with the banks to the mutual benefit of both.

Another way to deal with this problem is to ask your own banker to get the information for you. A banker will probably disclose more to another banker than he will to you, an outsider. Your banker will probably make a telephone call or two for you as an accommodation, but there is a limit to how many times he will do this, unless you keep large balances with him.

CREDIT BUREAUS AND REPORTING SERVICES

As an alternative or as a supplement to your own credit checking, you may want to use the services of credit bureaus and credit reporting services. They come in all shapes and sizes. You can buy a credit report for a little over a dollar or you can pay a thousand dollars—it depends upon how much information you want and how much time and effort it takes to get it.

The least expensive procedure and the one used by millions of retailers and other small businessmen is to become a member of the local credit bureau. The bureau is a membership organization that may be a cooperative, a nonprofit corporation, or a profit-making corporation. Generally there will be only one in your town or county, but there are over 2,000 throughout the country. The credit bureau keeps a computerized file of thousands (perhaps millions) of names of people living in its area, and through interchange arrangements it has access to similar files of other credit bureaus. Thus normally it can give you information not only on local residents but also on travelers passing through and also on people who have just moved to your area and have a credit record in another part of the country where they previously lived.

Credit bureau procedures are fairly standard. Normally a merchant or other businessman pays a yearly membership fee, which might be something like $50. When he wants to make an inquiry, he telephones the credit bureau, identifies himself by a prearranged code, and gives the name and address of his customer. (The bureau would like to have other information: name of employer, wife's name, Social Security number, previous address. The more information you can give them the easier it is to avoid mistakes or mistaken identities. But if all you have is a name and address, they will try to get a report for you.)

Most credit bureaus are highly automated in this computer age, and generally the person who answers the phone is sitting in front of a keyboard terminal with a display screen like a television set. The report can usually be summoned from the computer in a few seconds and displayed on the screen, and then it will be read to you on the phone. The charge may be something under $2 for each inquiry, no matter how much or little is turned up, and even if there is nothing in the computer the charge stands. Some credit bureaus give lower rates to volume users, some do not. If you want the report printed out and sent to you, there will be an additional charge.

The report will normally tell you the customer's employer; the name of his bank; a number of merchants, small-loan companies, and credit cards he has used; and whether his repayments have been satisfactory. Additional information on dependents, home ownership, other assets, and other income may or may not be in the file. Any history of the bankruptcy or civil or criminal litigation, including suits filed but never pressed, will appear.

The local credit bureau report provides just about the cheapest and fastest information you can get. It has a high degree of reliability and completeness, but not 100 percent. The credit bureau does not make any direct inquiry in response to your request. What it does is to maintain a gigantic file that receives inputs from merchants, small-loan companies, banks and other credit grantors, and court records. The accuracy and completeness of the information it receives will determine the accuracy and completeness of the information it will give you. Some businessmen are more conscientious than others about supplying inputs to the credit bureau; if the information is not submitted, the bureau will not seek it out. Normally your credit bureau membership will require you to submit information on your own credit customers.

The credit bureau report will tell you whether the individual has caused any credit or collection problems in the past or whether he has any litigation or criminal background. If there have been no problems reported to the bureau, it will simply tell you that everything has been satisfactory as far as it knows. In other words, it has received no critical reports from any of the credit sources that have reported to it.

The *best* thing it will tell you is that there is no bad news, but other than that, it won't give you any good news. It may tell you he owns his home, but it won't tell you his salary or his net worth.

In some cases you may decide that you want more information. You may find that you have not been successful in getting a clear idea of his net worth, his income, or what kind of work he does, or there may be something in his record or in his behavior that raises doubts in your mind. In this case, you may want to use a credit reporting service. Among the best-known national organizations in this field are Equifax (formerly Retail Credit Company) and TRW Credit Data, which provide reports on both individuals and businesses, and Dun and Bradstreet, which reports primarily on businesses.

A credit reporting agency will normally make a specific investigation in response to your request. Even if they have information in their files already, they will make some phone calls to bring the file up to date. These agencies usually charge something like $5 to $7 for their minimal report, which will give you information on employment, home ownership, experience with creditors, and other information in somewhat more depth and detail than the credit bureau report. This report usually includes a telephone call to the customer himself, unless you specify that you don't want the agency to contact him. The agency will not identify you; they will simply say that they are calling on behalf of a client. However, when the agency supplies information to you, you won't be able to tell whether it came from the customer himself or from an independent source.

If you don't belong to the credit bureau but would like to have their report, the credit reporting agency will get it for you for the credit bureau charge plus a service charge. If you want additional information beyond the minimum report, the charges vary according to how much time and effort is required. One major credit reporting agency charges $6 for its minimum report and will spend as much time beyond that as you want at $13.50 per hour ($15.50 in New York City). Much of their work consists of the exchange of information with other credit agencies and banks, together with what they can learn by a series of telephone calls to creditors, landlords, and merchants.

Credit reporting agencies are private, profit-making businesses. Unlike credit bureaus, they are not membership organizations. However, they won't let you buy a single $6 report. They have a minimum annual charge, which may be $100 or may be several hundred dollars.

Many states now have laws prohibiting credit agencies from asking for any information beyond the customer's record in paying what he owes. For example, they may ask a landlord whether the individual paid his rent on time, but they are not supposed to ask whether he held all-night parties or tore up the premises while he lived there. If you want this kind of information, or if you want to know about drinking or drug or sex habits, you will probably contact one of the credit reporting agencies that are also licensed to do private investigation. The investigation usually involves personal visits to make inquiry of neighbors, employers, co-workers, and others so as to get more complete information than will be given over the phone. It may cost $75 to $100 or possibly several hundred dollars.

You may find that the credit reporting agencies are useful to you. To a considerable degree they do the same thing that you could do yourself, which is to get on the phone and ask a lot of questions and get people talking as freely as possible. At least they will save you time. Beyond that, they are experienced in questioning people and coaxing information out of them, and they will probably get more information than you can get. And by virtue of their reciprocal arrangements with banks and other agencies they can sometimes get information that is not available to you.

Credit checking is necessary and important, but it will not guarantee that you won't have losses. Even if you learn everything you possibly can about your customer from all available sources, about his present circumstances and his past record, the future will still be uncertain. People change and circumstances change. A good past record provides a strong indication about future behavior, but extending credit is still taking a chance on a human being.

And when you are dealing with one of *those*, you never can be quite sure what to expect. . . .

SIX

———

How Can You Get
Insurance or Guarantees
Against Credit Losses?

*You Probably Can't / Insurance Companies / Credit Life
Insurance / Insurance Against Bad Checks*

YOU PROBABLY CAN'T

IT'S AS SIMPLE AS THAT. THE BIGGEST AND MOST SUCCESSFUL merchants and lenders and bankers in the world have credit losses, and so will you.

If you undertake to risk your capital in the hope that other people will keep their promises, promises that are enforceable only with difficulty and sometimes not at all, you will sometimes lose. Even though you know your customers well, even though you have personally made telephone calls to check on them and to verify their employment, their incomes, and their references, even though you have retained and paid a credit bureau or credit reporting agency to do additional checking to supplement your own—no matter how careful you are—you will have losses.

As has been emphasized earlier, it is important to remember that your credit customers are not malicious people or criminals who are out to steal from you. You will screen that type out fairly easily. Your credit customers will be basically honorable people with good intentions and *sincere* intentions. They tell you that they intend to pay and they really mean to pay. If they fail to pay, it is almost certainly because of bad luck or lack of will power or poor planning; either chance or human nature is the source of your problem. When you think about it, these are the causes of most of the things that can go wrong in your business.

INSURANCE COMPANIES

Since credit losses are very common, you might think that it would be possible to buy insurance against them, to pay somebody to guarantee you against losses. It is true that some insurance companies—a very few—will write insurance against credit losses, but only on a very limited and selective basis. Generally speaking this coverage is available only to manufacturers and wholesalers who sell to other businesses rather than to the general public. It is practically impossible for a retailer or small service business that deals with individuals to buy this insurance.

Even if the insurance company is willing to write the insurance, it will do so only on an individual basis. It will not even quote a premium until after it has made a thorough examination of the company's credit policies and its past experience and looked carefully at all of its accounts receivable. As a practical matter, this kind of insurance is probably available only to those companies whose credit policies are so tight and whose credit experience is so good that they don't really need the insurance.

Credit Life Insurance

Some lenders to consumers encourage the borrower to buy credit life and disability insurance—indeed, some lenders encourage it so vigorously that it is difficult for the borrower to resist the pressure. Credit life insurance provides that if the borrower should pass away while the obligation, or part of it, is still outstanding, the proceeds of the insurance policy will pay the debt in full. Similarly, if he should become disabled so that he can no longer earn a living, the insurance company will pay the debt.

This insurance is very common in connection with mortgage loans and automobile loans that run for three years or more. Credit life and disability insurance is group insurance that covers a large number of borrowers. Thus the premiums are low (compared with individual life insurance), and no physical examination is required.

A bank is glad to have credit life insurance covering a three- or four-year auto loan, because if the borrower dies after making 2½ years of payments, the bank is not interested in repossessing a 2½-year-old car. And they do not care to file a claim for a few hundred dollars against an estate that may not be settled for a couple of years. But credit life and disability insurance is of limited value to most businesses. They would have to absorb the premium, rather than passing it on to the borrower as the banks do. Moreover, bad debt and collection problems are rarely caused by death or disability. Rather they are caused by chance and the human failings of living and able-bodied people, where this insurance is of no value.

Insurance Against Bad Checks

Some businessmen might be interested in obtaining insurance against bad checks. A number of large banks have recently established systems that work like this: The merchant installs an electronic terminal, which is connected over a telephone line to the bank's computer. If the customer who wants to write a check happens to be a depositor in that particular bank and carries the bank's magnetically coded identification card, the merchant inserts the card in the terminal. If the system is working that day, he should get an answer within 20 seconds as to whether the customer's check is good. Some banks will immediately put a "hold" on that amount of money in the customer's account.

The merchant may pay something like $20 a month for this terminal and this service. This type of "debit card" program has been established by First National Bank of Atlanta, First National of Boston, Citibank in New York, and Wells Fargo in California, among others. Of course, this system doesn't help unless the customer has his account at the sponsoring bank.

Another check insurance program with broader application is operated by Telecredit, Inc., of Los Angeles. The participating merchant can call a toll-free (800) number and give the operator the customer's name, driver's license number, and date of birth. If the computer shows no bad-check problem for that individual, the operator then gives the merchant an identification number, and Telecredit insures that particular check up to $600. The cost to the merchant is 4 percent of the value of the check, with a $5 per month minimum for the service.

Credit Cards

*History of the Credit Card / Types of Credit Cards /
National Travel and Entertainment Cards / National Bank
Interchange System Cards / Local and Specialized, or
"Private-Label," Cards / Extent of Credit Card Owner-
ship / Advantages / Disadvantages*

I F YOU EXTEND CREDIT YOU WILL HAVE LOSSES. THAT IS,
unless you can get somebody to handle all the details of the
credit for you, including the losses. And it turns out that there is
somebody who is able, willing, and anxious to do this for you.
Or rather, several somebodies.

HISTORY OF THE CREDIT CARD

Shortly after the Second World War there appeared on the
American business scene that rarity of rarities, that wonder of
wonders, a genuinely new and constructive idea. An idea which
provided a valuable solution to a very common problem. A
real breakthrough.

The problem was that people wanted to be able to use credit
freely wherever they went. An increasing number of Americans, well into the tens of millions, had the kind of stable and
responsible economic behavior pattern which entitled them to
convenient credit with any merchant, restaurant, or purveyor
of goods or services. Their credit was well established at a certain bank and also at a few department stores, and perhaps
a restaurant or two. It was well established locally but it was
not easily *transferable.*

When this credible and creditable citizen went to a new
restaurant that he had never patronized before, he had to start

all over, so to speak, in the credit-verification process. Not a terribly difficult thing, to be sure, but time-consuming and sometimes somewhat embarrassing. It is not pleasant at the end of an enjoyable social dinner with a number of guests to have to keep them waiting while you hassle with the restaurant proprietor about accepting your credit or your check. It is difficult enough in your own home town, but it is much more difficult when you find yourself in a strange town where you have no charge accounts, where no bank knows you, and where it may be very difficult to get a personal check accepted.

Travelers' checks are of course useful, but they involve service charges and arranging to buy them before leaving on a trip. It seemed that there ought to be a better way. With tens of millions of credit-worthy individuals, it was a massive duplication of effort for every store and restaurant owner to have his own credit department, which required the individual to file a new credit request in each place he visited. Why isn't it possible, someone said, for one credit-granting agency to approve the individual's credit and communicate that approval to other creditors who might choose to do business with him?

Indeed, this technique has been used from time immemorial by people of wealth when they travel. Before leaving home they obtain a letter of introduction from their bank, which says something like, "Mr. so-and-so is well known to us as a responsible member of this community and as a valued client of our bank. We would appreciate any courtesies that can be extended to him." In other words, he will pay his bills and honor his checks, and if you in Paris have any concern about it, just contact your bank and they can contact us. Or if the letter of introduction was not enough, the traveler might take a letter of credit, which amounted to a guarantee that the bank itself would honor any obligations up to a certain amount. These personal letters of recommendation and credit were available only to people of the highest credit standing. They were not issued to the ordinary guy who lived from paycheck to paycheck, owed money on his car, and had $78.13 in his special checking account.

It seemed to make sense, then, for a central credit agency to take over the credit-granting function. This would be an enormous convenience for the general public. People would now be spared the necessity of establishing credit all over again every time they wanted to do business with a new restaurant or travel to a new city. It would also be beneficial for merchants, who were losing sales they might have made to travelers or strangers.

This alone was a major breakthrough. But it became even more dramatic when it was combined with another idea: the central agency would undertake the collection as well as the credit checking. The agency would not only say, "We have verified his credit standing—he is okay." This was a nice compliment to the individual, but one that still left to the merchant the job of collecting the money and also of *waiting* for it. The central agency then went much further; it put its money where its mouth was. It said, "Merchant, we have established his credit and we are so sure of it that we will pay you right away and we will collect from him later. And if we have any trouble collecting from him, that's our problem and not yours. You will have your money, and we won't ask for it back. If he is late in paying, we stand the delay and the interest cost. If he dies, we will file a claim against his estate. If he can't pay, or won't pay, or procrastinates or disappears, that is our worry, not yours."

And so the credit card was born in 1950.

TYPES OF CREDIT CARDS

Today there are three basic types of credit cards:

- national travel and entertainment cards
- national bank interchange system cards
- specialized and local or "private label" cards

National Travel and Entertainment Cards

The first of the travel and entertainment cards and the first national card was Diners Club. Originally, as its name implies, it concentrated on restaurants. Some years later American Express entered the field and then Carte Blanche. These three cards are commonly called travel and entertainment cards to distinguish them from the bank cards, but the name relates more to history than to present fact. American Express, Diners Club, and Carte Blanche are widely used in travel, dining, and entertainment, but they are widely used in other establishments, too.

American Express, Diners Club, and Carte Blanche all charge their cardholders a "membership" fee of $20 a year. They receive, process, and approve the credit application and then issue a card good for one year, usually with a dollar credit limit which the cardholder may not exceed in terms of total credit outstanding at any one time. Bills are sent to the cardholders once a month, and the bill is normally expected to be paid in full. In certain cases—airline tickets, for example—they offer an extended payment plan with a finance charge added, but the customer must specify at the time of purchase that he wants to pay that way.

These cards are anxious to have as many merchants as possible use their services. They undertake all collections from the cardholders and remit payment to the merchant, less a discount.

American Express, Diners Club, and Carte Blanche together have a total of about 10 million members. There is an unknown amount of duplication within this number; that is, some people carry two or all three. American Express, the largest of the three cards, is a major travel and financial services company operating throughout the world. Diners Club, originally an independent company, is now owned by Continental Corporation, an insurance and financial services holding company. Carte Blanche is a subsidiary of Avco Corporation.

The three so-called travel and entertainment cards were the first on the scene, but they have been overtaken by the bank cards, which are now much larger.

National Bank Interchange System Cards

In the case of the travel and entertainment cards, the credit card company handles every part of the transaction throughout the country. They sign up the card members, approve their credit, sign up the merchants, pay the merchants, and collect from the cardholders. The bank cards work somewhat differently, although the result is roughly the same for the cardholder and the merchant. Both deal with their local bank rather than with a national company.

There are still a few bank cards in certain localities, but there are only two national bank cards—Master Charge and BankAmericard. These two are not credit card companies but interchange and clearinghouse systems for the credit card activities of their bank members. Every major city and most smaller ones have one or more banks participating in the BankAmericard system and also one or more participating in the Master Charge system.

Each individual bank receives and processes credit card applications from individuals, who may be but need not be depositors in their bank. Once the credit is approved, the individual is issued a BankAmericard or a Master Charge card on the strength of the approval of that particular bank. The card may be used all over the country, but the member's home bank undertakes to collect from him and pay the merchant either directly or through the interchange system. The individual's home bank stands behind his credit and also stands ready to lend him money—or, to put it another way, to let him pay back what he owes over a period of months, with a finance charge, if he so desires.

Similarly, each merchant deals directly with a single member bank and receives all his payments from that bank for his sales on that card, less the discount. If the individual BankAmericard or Master Charge card was issued by another bank, perhaps in another part of the country, the merchant's home bank pays him and then collects from the cardholder's bank through the interchange organization.

The bank interchange system cards differ in three other ways from the so-called travel and entertainment cards. First, their credit standards are lower, and therefore they have issued many more cards; by the end of 1976 BankAmericard claimed 32 million members and Master Charge 38 million. The travel and entertainment cards have been oriented primarily toward upper-middle-income people and particularly toward businessmen who do a good deal of expense-account traveling and entertaining, and who presumably charge the $20 per year card fee to their employers or else take it as a business deduction on their income tax returns. The bank cards are much more readily available to ordinary working people with moderate incomes. Generally the principal requirements for a bank card are a reasonably good credit history and a steady job. Of course, the bank card will put a lower credit limit on its member than the travel and entertainment card.

The second major difference is that the travel and entertainment cards work like charge accounts, in that the holder is expected to pay his bill in full every month. The bank cards are like a revolving credit account. The cardholder has the opportunity to pay all at once or to stretch out his payments over a number of months; indeed, the bank not only gives him the opportunity to stretch out the payments but it actively encourages him to do this so that it can collect the finance charges. In the crazy world of credit, the cardholder who pays his bill right away is considered a freeloader because he has deprived the bank of the chance to earn interest on installment payments. The bank's attitude is, in effect, "Now that we've gone to all this trouble to establish your credit and issue this card to you, the least you can do is use it on a time-payment basis and let us earn some interest. That's what we're in business for, you know."

The third major difference is that American Express, Diners Club, and Carte Blanche charge their cardholders $20 a year, while the bank interchange cards usually charge nothing, with a few exceptions. Under the bank interchange system, each member bank has the right to set its own terms in dealing with both cardholders and merchants. BankAmericard advises that as of the end of 1975 two of the 6,752 banks that sponsor their card levied annual fees upon the cardholder. And New York's Citibank imposes a minimum 50-cent finance charge on each monthly statement with a balance outstanding and owing; that is, they are going after the "freeloaders" described above. If the cardholder pays on time with finance charges, fine; if he pays in full within 30 days he must pay a minimum 50-cent charge. Now that the bank interchange cards have built a large cardholder base, it is possible that other member banks will begin to impose annual fees or minimum finance charges.

Local and Specialized, or "Private Label," Cards

In addition to BankAmericard and Master Charge there are still a few local bank cards in certain areas. Most of these were established before the rapid growth of BankAmericard and Master Charge. In general it is fair to say that the banks that have their own local cards are looking for a graceful way to abandon them without losing face. The card of an Atlanta bank is of limited usefulness when the cardholder is visiting San Diego. BankAmericard and Master Charge have an enormous advantage over local bank cards in that they are accepted all over the United States without question, and they are increasingly accepted in Canada and overseas, too. For this reason it seems to be a fairly good guess that local bank cards will ultimately disappear and leave the field to the Big Two.

In addition to travel and entertainment cards and bank interchange cards, there are a number of specialized or "private label," cards. These are really nothing more than conventional charge accounts (either single-pay or installment) that now use plastic cards which are the same size as other credit cards and may or may not carry a magnetic code. Some of these are national in scope, such as the airlines, major gasoline retailers, car rental companies, and some hotel chains. In addition, many of the better department and specialty stores that cater to upper-middle-income people have issued credit cards to their charge account holders. Sometimes the issuing merchant or company handles its own credit; sometimes it turns the whole credit operation over to a bank without the customer knowing about it.

EXTENT OF CREDIT CARD OWNERSHIP

By the end of 1976 BankAmericard and Master Charge claimed a total of 70 million cardholders, and the number continues to increase by several million per year. There are about 10 million travel and entertainment cards and an unknown but very large number of private label cards; the gasoline companies alone may have close to 100 million outstanding. All together there are probably close to 200 million credit cards floating around in the United States, and more abroad.

Because of duplication it is impossible to know exactly how many people carry credit cards. A well-traveled businessman may carry at least one travel and entertainment card and one or both bank cards, together with several private label cards. Almost all issuers of credit cards encourage customers to obtain additional cards for other members of the family. Thus, the upper-middle-income businessman's wife will probably carry at least one travel and entertainment card and perhaps several department store cards. And older children may have cards, too. This family might have as many as fifteen or twenty cards, while a factory worker with a special checking account might have only one in the family.

One of the bank interchange cards claims in its promotional material that at least 44 percent of all U.S. households have either BankAmericard or a Master Charge card and that in families with incomes of over $8,000 the percentage is 60 percent. Professor of Marketing Roger D. Blackwell of Ohio State University sent questionnaires to 1,000 households with incomes over $4,000 and learned that 80 percent of them had some type of credit card.

Precise numbers are not available, but it is clear that the use of credit cards is continuing to grow, with the bank interchange cards growing the fastest. It is also clear that a high and increasing proportion of the more affluent and more stable people carry credit cards and have become accustomed to using them regularly and routinely. And these are your most attractive and most profitable customers.

ADVANTAGES

Credit cards are here to stay, because they make sense. They have virtually eliminated the enormous duplication of effort involved when many different merchants went through the same questioning, verification, and credit-approval process. They have vast experience in credit checking and processing, and they do it in huge volume; therefore, they do it as efficiently and as successfully as anybody can and considerably more efficiently than most merchants can do it for themselves. The organization that specializes in credit and has a number of people working full time at it is bound to do a better job than a businessman who handles credit only a few hours a week as only one of his many chores. While you are groping in the dark, so to speak, they have it down to a system.

What about lost or stolen cards or cards that have been canceled? What about the cardholder who exceeds his maximum credit? Normally the credit card organization takes these losses and the merchants do not. There are some exceptions, however. They publish and distribute at regular intervals lists of cards that are unacceptable for some reason, and the merchant is expected to consult this list before approving credit. The merchant is also expected to compare the signature on his sales slip with the signature on the card in order to detect obvious forgeries—a surprising number of businessmen fail to do this. Also, the credit card company will normally impose a house limit on each merchant (say, $50 or $100 per transaction) and require him to check by telephone before writing a ticket in excess of that amount. Occasionally disputes arise between merchants and the credit card organization as to whether the merchant took the proper precautions.

We have said that the major costs of credit are money and time—the money cost in losses, the loss of interest on your money while you are waiting to be paid, and the other out-of-pocket costs of credit—such as expense of printing forms, of telephone calls to check credit, of credit bureau and credit agency fees and collection costs. And the time, energy, and hassle involved in credit checking, credit decisions, dunning, and collections. You will save practically all this money and time if you turn over your credit operations to one or more of the credit card systems.

Furthermore, the credit card people will pay you considerably faster than your customer in most cases. The bank cards generally will allow you to deposit your BankAmericard or Master Charge slips in your bank account and to draw on the funds within two days. The travel and entertainment cards used to pay once a month, but they now offer a variety of plans for reimbursing the merchant. By adding ½ or 1 percentage point to his discount, the merchant can be paid within days instead of weeks.

Another possibility is that your customer may put you pretty far down on his priority list. If he has a lot of bills and can't pay all of them, he is likely to put his light bill, his phone bill, his rent or mortgage payment, and his bank and credit card payments ahead of you. Failure to pay these may have serious effects in his life or on his credit rating, and so they take precedence over what he owes you.

One merchant had this to say:

> . . . I used to carry my own charge accounts for my women's apparel shop. That involved keeping daily records, printing statements, mailing hundreds of letters monthly, writing off bad debts, and borrowing on short-term notes to pay my bills because of money owed to me by customers. In short, I was a banker, lending money to the public (at no interest) out of my own pocket.
>
> Three years ago I switched all charge sales to bank credit cards. The results were astonishing. Charges made on my bank cards are only about 10 percent of my total business, versus about 30 percent under my old system. And my costs are a fraction of what they were. . . .
>
> —Letter from K.P., Marquette, Mich.,
> published in *Consumer Reports*,
> May 1976.

DISADVANTAGES

The writer expresses a point of view that deserves serious consideration. Of course, credit cards cost something, too. That something is the discount.

When the national credit card organization reimburses you for your sales slip, they will discount it by a percentage that may run as high as 5½ percent or as low as 3 percent. Most smaller merchants will pay at least 4½ to 5 percent.

It is difficult to say exactly what your discount might be, because it is determined according to the volume of business you do with the particular card, and with some cards it may vary according to how fast you are reimbursed. Also, one of the bank cards adjusts its formula according to the size of your average ticket. They claim that it costs them 32 cents to process every ticket and that therefore they would lose money on a

$5 sale even if they charged you 6 percent. They will give a better deal (lower discount) to the merchant whose average sale is $75 or $100 than to the one whose average is $10.

One further piece of bad news is that the discount normally is applied to the total amount of the sales check, including tips, sales taxes, federal excise tax, and anything else that happens to be included.

The travel and entertainment cards are centrally administered by a single organization, and they say they have a standard fee that applies throughout the country. It is a formula that depends upon the total volume of business you do on their card, but there is one formula for restaurants, a different one for most other retailers, a different one for hotels, and so on. Asking the credit card company for the formula is something like asking for military secrets; it seems clear that there is a certain amount of room for negotiation. Furthermore, the travel and entertainment cards have reduced their discounts in response to the very effective competition from the bank interchange cards.

Since the bank interchange systems serve their member banks, there is no national formula for discounts. Rather, each individual bank sets the discount for merchants it contracts with.

The discount is painful, but it represents just about all your credit cost. The credit card organization will supply you with application forms, promotional material, and decals for your door or window, and sometimes they do some advertising, too. At this writing, American Express is offering promotional discounts to cardholders in some parts of the country who patronize restaurants on their card.

You will have to have an imprinting machine, but since all credit cards are the same size, you will only need one. You can buy it for $35 or $40, or one of the bank card systems will rent it to you for 50 cents a month. The only other cost would be losses sustained by you where the credit card company claims that you were careless in checking signatures or failed to telephone for verification when you were supposed to and disputes do arise.

The view expressed here is that the credit card discount,

painful though it will be, costs you less than the combined cost in time and money of handling your own credit. However, there are certain other disadvantages to credit cards.

First, some people don't have credit cards. They are in the minority, and the minority is getting smaller all the time, but it will not disappear. If you grant credit only through a national credit card, you may lose a sale to a credit-worthy individual who does not carry that particular card. But perhaps this lost sale should not concern you too much. Most of the more affluent people and the better credit risks carry at least one card, and therefore the credit risk in selling to nonholders tends to be rather high. The nonholding group includes a number of irresponsible and undependable people, unemployed people, people who have applied for cards and have been turned down, and people who have had their cards revoked because of delinquency and misuse.* They are not a very promising group for you to extend credit to, anyway.

A second disadvantage is that, unless you are very careful, you tend to lose track of your regular customers. If you handle your own charge accounts, you will have a complete and up-to-date list of most of your best customers, and you will always know the status of their accounts with you. You can keep in touch with them by sending them promotional literature and announcements of sales.

But this is not an insuperable obstacle. With a little paper work you can compile and maintain a permanent list of names and addresses of every cardholder who has been a customer. (You will have to ask for his address, since that does not appear on the plastic card.) Then you will know how to communicate with your regular customers.

There is another imaginative way to deal with your preferred customers. You can take them aside and tell them that they are especially valued customers and you want them to have the privilege of shopping on credit without using the credit card if they care to. What you are doing here is to skim off the cream

---

* There is another small but growing group of nonholders: the people who find themselves lacking in self-discipline, who constantly get in over their heads. Then they tear up all their cards to try to restore some order to their personal affairs.

of your credit card customers, those who give you the most business and the most profit and those who are certain to pay their bills. They will be flattered by the special treatment, and you will save the discount on their purchases.

The credit card companies do not encourage this approach, but they admit that it may make sense for you to use your own credit in combination with theirs. In fact, they are making a strong promotional effort with prestigious department stores, urging them to keep their own credit programs but to add the bank card as a supplementary program to bring new customers into their stores.

The 3⅜-by-2⅛-inch plastic card that was introduced by Diners Club in 1950 has long since achieved a prominent and permanent place in the American business scene. And it is still growing. The system is not perfect and it is not foolproof, and it certainly isn't free, but on balance it may offer the most practical way for you to handle credit.

Should You Give Discounts for Cash?

*Economic Justification / New Federal Laws
and Regulations*

THE ENORMOUS INCREASE IN THE USE OF CREDIT CARDS HAS produced a major change in the way Americans do business, particularly in retail trade and in service businesses. The credit card has made it possible for many smaller retailers to offer credit for the first time, especially those who don't have the ability, the inclination, or the time to handle credit themselves.

As mentioned in previous chapters, credit may help you build your business. Alternatively, you may find that you have to offer credit because your competition gives you no choice. In any event, credit costs you money, and you will almost certainly pass on the cost to your customers in the form of higher prices. This is a legitimate and proper business practice, and indeed you would be very foolish if you did not raise your prices to cover the cost of credit. Otherwise you would see your profit margins drastically reduced and perhaps they would disappear entirely.

For example, suppose that you make a profit of 8 cents on every dollar of sales, after all costs and expenses, including your own compensation. If you participate in a credit card program and pay 4 percent of sales to the credit card people, you have cut your profit margin in half. (Or perhaps you have cut it by slightly more than that, because the credit card discount applies to sales taxes, too.) If you make only 4 or 5 percent on your sales dollar, your profit will be just about wiped out by the credit card discount. And a 4 to 5 percent margin is not unusual in retailing; in fact, some retailers make even less than that.

Thus your selling prices are certain to include something for the cost to you of extending and handling credit and collections. And if you change from a cash-only policy to credit, you will have to raise prices.

Some of your customers will be smart enough to realize that you have the cost of credit built into your pricing. And some of them may object to it. It is a legitimate business practice, and if all of your customers buy on credit, then they are all treated fairly. They are all using a service and paying for it.

However, suppose you extend credit to some customers while others pay cash. (This, of course, is very common both in retailing and in other businesses.) Now a potential problem arises. Your cash customer may complain that he is paying for a service that he does not care to use. He may contend that he should not have to pay for credit that benefits your other customers but does not benefit him. And he may ask for a discount for paying cash.

ECONOMIC JUSTIFICATION

One thing that makes this troublesome is that the request is not an unreasonable one. It has a good deal of economic justification measured in dollars and cents—you know that and your customer may know it, too. The practice of extending credit to some customers and giving discounts for cash is a very common and very widespread practice in business transactions at the manufacturing and wholesale level. In fact, it is practically universal.

Much of the business in this country is conducted on what is called a "2/10, net/30" basis. This means that the bill is supposed to be paid in full 30 days after the goods are shipped; anything over 30 days is considered a slow or past-due payment. Moreover, as an incentive for prompt payment, the seller permits the buyer to take a 2 percent discount if he pays within ten days.

Sometimes even higher discounts are arranged by negotiation. The seller gets his money faster and is spared the necessity of repeated billing and worrying about whether he will get his money. These trade discounts are only partially justified by the interest factor, since 2 percent is a pretty high interest rate for a period of 20 or 30 days or so. The principal justification is peace of mind, of having the payment in hand rather than worrying about when—or whether—it will be received.

The customer who asks for a discount for paying cash is, of course, telling you that you may lose the sale if you refuse to give it to him. And if you send him away unsatisfied this time, he will probably never come back. What makes this more serious is that he is not alone. He is one of a fairly sizable group of sophisticated shoppers who do not want to pay for credit that they don't use and have a pattern of shopping at cash-only or discount stores.

This group of people might give you substantial amounts of business. Some of them will ask you for a discount for cash. But most of them will probably not ask—they will simply stay away. Thus, if you give discounts for cash, you may attract a number of customers who would not otherwise do business with you.

As a sensible businessman you obviously have no enthusiasm for adopting what amounts to a dual pricing policy—one price for your credit customers and a lower price for your cash customers. There are enough problems and complications in your business without adding this one. But as often happens in the competitive world, you may have no real choice. Those customers who refuse to pay extra for credit are a large and growing group, and there are signs that the demand for discounts for cash is becoming one of the major objectives of consumer activists. As credit cards become more widely used, the demand for discounts for cash is likely to become more vocal and more insistent.

NEW FEDERAL LAWS AND REGULATIONS

The legal aspects of discounts for cash changed rather dramatically in 1975. Until that time, many credit card companies had provisions in their contracts with merchants that *prohibited* them from giving a discount to a cash customer. A number of lawsuits were brought in an attempt to invalidate these provisions, and then they were rendered null and void by the Fair Credit Billing Act of 1975. This new federal law makes it illegal for a credit card company or anybody else to interfere with or restrain a merchant's freedom to offer lower prices to cash customers.

The new law does not *require* you to give discounts for cash, but it *permits* it. And as people become aware of this new legislation, it is likely that the demand for discounts for cash will become more and more common. Dual pricing may become widespread.

It is not yet clear how this law will be administered and enforced, because the regulations under the law have not yet been issued by the Federal Reserve Board. However, the FRB has put forward for comment one proposed regulation that could very much complicate the picture. It would require that if you offer a discount for cash to any customer, you must offer it to all customers, and you must post a sign to that effect. If this regulation is adopted, which seems likely, and if it is vigorously enforced, which seems impossible, it could deprive you of the opportunity of favoring your valued customers with exclusive and special treatment.

———

Now You Have to Worry About Collecting

Record-Keeping / Using Your Records / The Grace Period / What Next?

Now you've gone and done it . . . you have given credit, you have turned over valuable merchandise in exchange for promises.

This is virtually the same as lending money, so now you are in the banking business, so to speak. And now, just like a banker, you have to worry about getting paid.

You probably knew that there would be problems with collections, that the money wouldn't just roll in automatically. But you may not be prepared for how hard it really is. Collecting what is owed to you is a big job, a hard job, a time-consuming job. It takes a lot of work, a lot of attention, a lot of thought. And worry. Especially worry. You may find that the worry takes more out of you than anything else.

Post-mortems, among other things. Did you make a mistake to give credit to this one? Or that one? Are you having second thoughts? Do you remember some doubts, some vague uneasiness that you dismissed at the time but now seems to loom larger?

You will probably not spend much time with second thoughts about the customers you turned down for credit, but you will worry a great deal about those you approved. Because now you are stuck with them, you are close to them, you have an intense interest in their well-being. You are in a sense partners with them until they pay.

RECORD-KEEPING

What else do you do about collections, in addition to worrying? The first thing you will do, and it is absolutely essential that you do it, is to compile and maintain accurate records. You must have excellent information on your customer receivables. Your records must be detailed, accurate, and complete, and they must be kept up to date at all times. You should know exactly how much each customer owes you at any given moment. Each individual file must be kept current so that it reflects payments as soon as they are made. There is almost nothing you can do that will anger a customer more than to dun him about a bill he has already paid, or to tell him that he owes you more than he actually does.

The file must also be kept completely current with respect to additional purchases. You must know every day exactly and currently how much he owes you. Remember that many people are good for $100 but can be serious problems if they owe $1,000. If you do business with a customer two or three times a week, his credit can get out of hand in less than a month unless you stay on top of it and know exactly how much he owes you at any given time.

Here are some suggestions for record-keeping:

- For each credit customer, establish a permanent individual customer record, which is maintained separately from your sales slips and invoices.
- The individual customer record should show the date, invoice number, and amount of each new purchase.
- It should show a running balance of the total amount owed and the date or dates—"on or about"—when you expect payments to be received.
- It should show the date and amount of each payment actually received.
- It should show the date and amount of monthly bills sent by you, of reminders, of collection letters, of telephone

or face-to-face conversations about the account or about your business with him. In fact, it should contain a brief notation of any and every contact of any kind with that customer.

- You should assign to one individual the responsibility for keeping these records. It doesn't have to be you; this is a clerk's job. It must be done accurately, but any careful clerk can handle it. But only one person should have the responsibility. (If you have several people doing it on different days or at different times, some of it is bound to be lost or overlooked. Each one thought the other took care of posting yesterday's sales.) It is *your* responsibility to watch that clerk closely, to make sure that he carries out *his* responsibility, and to crack the whip when necessary. Each purchase and payment should be entered in the individual customer record the same day as it occurs, or the next business day at the very latest.

It is vitally important that these individual customer credit records be kept very carefully, very accurately, very completely. And very currently. You cannot even begin to manage your credit and collections properly without really first-class record-keeping. These are probably the most important and most valuable records you have in your business.*

USING YOUR RECORDS

All right. Now that you have set up an efficient system and have somebody responsible for keeping the credit records up to date, the next point is that *you have to look at the records.* The best files in the world are worthless if they are kept in a drawer that is never opened. You have to study them carefully, review them, and think about them. You have to *use* the information.

Reviewing your receivables is an important part of your

---

* A famous business cartoon of two generations ago showed a building on fire and the owner of a business jumping out the window into the firemen's net below. In the haste of leaving he had time to take only one thing with him, and he carries under his arm a box labeled "accounts receivable."

entrepreneurial and managerial responsibility. It should not be something that you do occasionally, when you have a few minutes free or when you get around to it after everything else is done. Good receivables can turn into overdue ones and then into collection problems and then into losses while you are preoccupied with other aspects of running your business.

You should establish a regular schedule for review of receivables either by you or by one of your partners or someone capable of making managerial decisions. This is *not* a clerical job, not a job for a junior employee, but for one of the bosses. And it should be done by one person, because only when that person conducts the review regularly over a period of months does he begin to detect patterns of purchase and payment and then deviations from the pattern that spell potential trouble. The review should be conducted once a week, and it is highly desirable that it be scheduled at the same time every week so as to build and continually reinforce a habit.

The purpose of the review is to separate out the potential problems, to identify them as early as possible, and then to focus attention on them, to think about them, and to decide what steps should be taken. Problems with overdue accounts rarely go away by themselves, and they almost never become smaller as time passes. On the contrary, they usually become larger and more serious with the passage of time. Therefore, it is absolutely essential to identify them early and to start worrying about them early.

This is an extremely important point. The further behind you let the customer get, the greater the risk that you will never collect at all. The most recent receivables are the best ones. All authorities on credit agree that the difficulty of collection increases in direct proportion to the age of the account. In credit departments of large companies, it is standard practice to classify accounts according to age—current, 30 days overdue, 60 days overdue, and so on.

When you originally reached an understanding with the customer about credit, you undoubtedly had some discussion with him about the terms and the time of payment that you expected. Perhaps you are fortunate enough to have a single repayment schedule for all your customers. (And if they all stick to it, you are really fortunate.) Whatever the payment pattern is supposed to be, each customer will probably deviate somewhat from it. You will want to note in the records what the payment schedule is supposed to be. And you will also note what *this* customer's payment pattern has been in the past as a guide to what you may expect in the future.

Your records will show the expected payment date for each customer, based on your original understanding with him as modified by his particular pattern of payment as you have observed it over the months and years. Noting the expected payment date will save you a great deal of time and needless worry. If the pattern indicates that you should expect payment next week, there is nothing to worry about now. If payment is expected this week and hasn't come in yet, the name goes on the "watch the mail" list. If payment was expected last week and hasn't come in yet, that name goes on the "worry" list.

Assuming that your record-keeping system is set up properly and maintained efficiently, it will be a routine clerical matter to establish the worry list. Deciding what action to take is, on the contrary, not a routine matter at all, but a difficult judgmental one. As is almost always true when dealing with human beings, there is no simple rule or formula.

THE GRACE PERIOD

Probably there should be some sort of grace period for most customers. That is, if they go a week or two beyond the expected payment date, you will have them on your worry list, but you will probably not do anything about it or say anything to them during a reasonable grace period. (For example, in life insurance policies it is customary to provide a 30-day grace period for payment of premiums. Some people make a habit of using the grace period and paying all of their premiums three or three and a half weeks past the due date.)

You may find that you have a small number of troublesome customers who have caused you concern repeatedly and do not deserve a grace period. Where the performance and personality of a customer point to this conclusion, you should not hesitate to implement it. In such a case you will start taking action within a day or two after the date the payment was expected. You will probably have only a few like this, but there is no reason why they should not be singled out for special treatment.

And, in general, you probably shouldn't make the grace period too long. If your customer ever gets the idea that you are going to let him off the hook, you are in real trouble. The first reminder, the first needle, is an important one, because it serves notice that you are aware of the debt, that you haven't overlooked it and you don't intend to. It is not unreasonable to send him or give him some kind of nudge when he is ten days to two weeks overdue. There is a saying among credit men, "If you forget, the debtor isn't going to remember."

WHAT NEXT?

Now. All reasonable grace periods have expired. You are worrying more and more, and payment still hasn't come in. What do you do next?

Collection Letters

*Early Reminders / Printed Form Versus Personal Letter /
Sample Letters / Characteristics of the Collection Letter /
Friendliness / Sympathy / Apology / Flexibility / Firm-
ness / Briefness / Collection Letters Avoid Confrontation*

OUR MODERN WORLD IS FILLED WITH SOPHISTICATED ELEC-
tronic communications devices. We send and receive
messages by telegraph, telephone, television, radar, and citizens'
band radio. Your sales clerk can push buttons on an electronic
credit terminal in your store and get a message back in seconds.

These devices are useful for rapid communication, but when
it comes to collection of past-due accounts, one of the most
effective techniques is a very old-fashioned one: the personal
letter. It is direct, it gets attention, and it makes unmistakably
clear the seriousness of the matter. It can be tailored to the
personalities of the creditor and the customer and to the
urgency of the demand.

It is probably the most important and most widely used collection technique. It is the only collection method used by
some businesses, and every credit business will use it sooner
or later. If you run your business alone, you may say, "I don't
have hot and cold running secretaries around here, I can't
be bothered with letter writing." Still, there will be many occa-
sions when you should use either a printed notice or a personal
letter to needle your nonpaying and slow-paying customers.
Sometimes you will see them, sometimes you will telephone
them, but eventually you may have to write a letter. Or two
letters. Or three . . .

Somebody once said that the goal of a system of taxation should be to pluck the maximum number of feathers from the goose with the minimum of squawking. The objective of a collection letter is something like that—to bring in a check as soon as possible without irritating the customer any more than is absolutely necessary. He might be a good customer in the future, possibly even a very good one. Maybe he is late now because of a temporary problem that will soon clear up.

The collection effort is a sequential one. You don't choose one technique and use it over and over. Rather, you use a step-by-step approach in which each step varies and escalates slightly from the previous one. If the first step does the job and brings in the payment, fine. But if it doesn't, you move to step two. And so on.

EARLY REMINDERS

Your first letter or notice and perhaps your second will be in the nature of friendly requests or reminders. If it is necessary to move to later steps in the sequence, the friendliness will gradually disappear and will be replaced by firmness, which increases until it becomes a demand. And in the final stages you may have to use deadlines and threats.

One approach to the early stages of the collection effort is to send another copy of the bill with the addition of the words "Past Due" or "Second Request." The next month the notice becomes more insistent; for example, "Two months overdue; please remit now."

This message can be added to the bill with a rubber stamp or written by hand, and it's a good idea to use a different color of ink. Many large companies are now programming their computers to add these words to the printout of the bill. However, it can be argued that this is less effective than a rubber stamp wielded by a human being or a handwritten notice.

PRINTED FORM VERSUS PERSONAL LETTER

There are differences of opinion about whether to use printed forms or cards as collection notices, rather than personal letters. It is becoming increasingly common to use these printed materials. You will have to make your own judgment based on the type of people who owe you money and the kind of relationship you have with them.

If your debtor is a large corporation and your reminder ends up with a clerk in a large accounts-payable department, he is not likely to be impressed at all by the wording, or by the fact that the notice comes in the form of an individually typed letter with a personal signature as opposed to a printed form.

SAMPLE LETTERS

If you are a retailer dealing with charge account customers, you may find that the printed notice is just as effective and costs you a great deal less than an individual letter. A fairly common approach is to prepare and print four or five collection notices making up a sequence of increasing severity and decreasing friendliness. Something like this:

#1:

IT'S EASY

to forget to pay a bill. That's probably what you did about the last bill we sent you. You forgot.

Now we have the unpleasant task of reminding you that your account is overdue. If you haven't already done so, please be good enough to send us your check for $_____ as soon as possible.

#2:

WE ARE PLEASED TO SERVE YOU

as a credit customer. We hope you have found our service satisfactory. On our part, we have found our relationship with you to be a pleasant one in the past and we hope it will be pleasant again in the future.

But right now it isn't, because you aren't holding up your end of our understanding. You are not being fair to us by waiting so long to pay us.

You owe $_____. Send us your check, please. Today!

#3:

NOW REALLY . . . YOU ARE EXPECTING TOO MUCH

if you think we will just forget about what you owe.

Your account is long overdue. You are abusing the credit we extended to you. We have shown every courtesy and as much patience as humanly possible, but you have ignored our reminders.

As you know, the amount due is $_____.

Please send your check WITHOUT FURTHER DELAY!

#*4*:

WE CAN'T TAKE ANY MORE OF THIS.

We have bent over backwards to be patient and reasonable about the $_____ you owe us, but it doesn't seem to do any good.

Therefore, if we don't have your check by _____, MORE DRASTIC ACTION WILL BE TAKEN.

#*5*:

FINAL NOTICE BEFORE SUIT.
$_____

If you decide to use this approach, there are a number of things you can do to overcome the impersonal aspect of the printed card or form. First, the exact amount owed should be filled in by hand so that the customer is certain that there is no mistake. It is not a bad idea to write the customer's name by hand at the top. The notice should be sent by first-class mail, because people sometimes assume that third-class mail is advertising matter and throw it away without opening it. Also, the extra few cents of postage show that you take the matter seriously and that you expect him to do the same.

Another trick that you might use occasionally is to send the notice first-class in a plain envelope, with the address written by hand and with no return address or identifying mark on the envelope. Most of the mail that people get contains no surprises; they can tell what it is before they open it. The unusual letter that cannot be identified from the envelope arouses considerable curiosity and carries an air of mystery; thus, it gets much more attention and makes a more vivid impression.

CHARACTERISTICS OF THE COLLECTION LETTER

The collection process involves a sequence or series of efforts, each a little different from the last. With appropriate adjustments in various stages of the sequential pattern, a good

collection notice or letter should have the following characteristics:

Friendly	*and*	Sympathetic, Sorrowful, and
Flexible, Firm.	*but*	
	And	Short.

Friendliness

A good business relationship is based upon good will and
mutual satisfaction, not upon contracts and the assertion of
legal rights. When you extended credit in the first place you were
showing friendship and trust. The collection effort should be a
continuation of this friendly approach, at least in the early
stages. Eventually you may have to become unfriendly, but
you will postpone that as long as you can, and you hope to
avoid it entirely.

If you meet the customer to discuss what he owes you, you
will smile and say hello before getting down to business, and
your collection letter or notice should do the same.

Anothing thing. Your language should be casual and informal. The old stilted language of business correspondence ("Reference is made to our invoice of the 10th instant") has gone out
with the high starched collar—and good riddance to both.

Your letter is not a legal treatise. You should express yourself pretty much as you would if you were talking to the customer face to face or on the phone. Simplicity and directness
and informality are important; syntax and elaborate verbiage
are not.

Sympathy

Your letter should be gentle and kind—at first. It should
show sympathy and understanding. You are human, too, and
you realize that people sometimes forget things, or have a run
of bad luck, or have trouble sticking to a budget. While you
are concerned about the failure of your trusted customer to pay
on time, you are confident that there is some good reason for

this, and if he will tell you the reason you will surely be understanding about it.

Your letter should avoid showing unfriendliness or distrust by making an accusation of any kind. You may suspect the customer's truthfulness or his motives, but you will not say so. On the contrary, you will bend over backwards to find excuses for him. For example:

- Possibly our bill—or your check—was lost in the mail . . .
- At this busy holiday season, you may have forgotten . . .
- We know you didn't intentionally overlook . . .
- Perhaps there is some misunderstanding about the terms of your revolving account. . . .
- Frankly, we are puzzled. There must be some good reason why a trusted and valued customer like yourself has failed . . .

Apology

In keeping with the friendly and sympathetic approach, your letter should express regret that it is necessary to communicate an unpleasant message to a trusted customer and friend. You wish you didn't have to do this—you'd rather talk about pleasant, happy things.

You are writing more in sorrow than in anger. The customer undoubtedly intended to pay on time. Perhaps illness or some other misfortune has befallen him, and if so you would be saddened.

You are sorry to have to bring up an unpleasant matter, you are sorry if things have not gone well for him, and you are also sorry that the trust you placed in him may not have been deserved.

You are sorry, but—and this is a very important point—*you are not apologetic.* You do not have to apologize for asking for money that is owed to you and insisting that it be paid. Your expression of regret is an expression of civility, of politeness. It troubles you to have to speak of such things to a friend, but it will trouble you a great deal more if he doesn't pay his bill.

The amount is due and payable, and you want it paid—let there be no mistake about that. This is no time to talk about the quality of the merchandise, or whether he should have bought it. And you certainly don't want it returned. The purchase is completed, the money is owed, and it must be paid.

Flexibility

Although you must press him for payment, you would like to make things as easy as possible for him. You know he's not dishonest, that he intends to pay, and you are willing to discuss and consider a variety of ways that he might do it. If you could know the reason for the delay, you would be happy to sit down with him and try to work out some sensible way to resolve the matter.

He expects a creditor to threaten him, and he is prepared for that, but you can disarm him by telling him that you don't want to make things tougher for him, you just want to help. If he can't pay it all now, maybe he can pay some of it. (If you haven't heard from him for several months, and you don't know whether he has died or gone to Brazil, you will be quite pleased to get a check for half of what he owes, or even a quarter.) If he can't pay anything right now, you can talk about setting up a schedule that he can meet.

Flexibility works both ways—there is no reason why you cannot suggest a schedule of delayed payments with interest added. After all, this customer now has two obligations to you. One is the original amount owed and the second is the amount that the delay is costing you. The assumption was that he would pay in 30 days; since he has not done so, you are losing interest on the money and it is reasonable to ask him to pay it.

Some stores have improved their collections by informing slow-pay customers that they have "adopted a new policy" of imposing interest or service charges on past-due accounts. The delinquent customer is hardly in a position to protest this, and he rarely does. The opportunity to avoid an additional charge may goad him into action. Also, it is quite possible that he has money in the savings bank earning interest while he is keeping you waiting and *costing* you interest.

Firmness

The friendliness and sympathy, the sorrow and the flexibility constitute an effort to disarm, to win the customer over with kindness, to appeal to his better instincts. These efforts are important, but they are incidental. The central purpose of the letter or notice is to insist upon payment and to threaten additional action if it is not received.

Remember, your letter, for all its friendliness, is not a request, not a plea. It is a demand.

In the early stages of the collection sequence, the threats are only implied or hinted at. Later they become more explicit. For example:

Sometimes other stores ask for information about our charge account customers. If we should get such a call today about you, we would have to answer that you are running very late. . . .

Or deadlines are added:

If we don't get some kind of word from you in seven days, we will turn your account over to our collection agency. We sincerely hope you will enable us to avoid this unpleasantness. . . .

People are becoming increasingly aware of the fact that an unfavorable credit report can haunt them for many years, perhaps for the rest of their lives. With some customers, this approach can be very persuasive:

We are a member of the _____ Credit Bureau, and our contract with them requires us to report to them when we have unfavorable credit experience with any of our customers. Because you are now _____ months past due, we will have to send a negative report to the bureau if we don't hear from you by October _____.

Some credit bureaus supply their members with form letters that the retailer can send out on the letterhead of the credit bureau. For example:

We (credit bureau) have been advised by ___(store)___ that your account is overdue in the amount of $_____. We suggest that you settle this matter at once so that we may remove this information from our files. . . .

On the other hand, don't overdo it. You are entitled to insist that your money be paid to you and to specify what lawful steps you may take if you have to. But you should not cross the line into abuse or harassment. You may be surprised to know that even a legitimate demand for payment may conceivably constitute the crime of extortion if it is stated in extreme or violent terms. "Pay up or I'll break your knees" is the language of hoodlums, not of businessmen.

Briefness

You don't have to use great clouds of words in your collection letter. Remember that your basic message is very simple: "Please pay up—now!" The friendliness and civility take more words, but not that many more. You don't want to bring up extraneous matters or give the customer an opportunity to change the subject or divert attention from the matter at hand. A brief and direct statement is best.

Under no circumstances should a collection letter go beyond a page, and usually two or three short paragraphs are sufficient. Sometimes only one sentence, or even a fragment of a sentence, can be effective:

"There must be a good reason why you haven't paid us for four months. Can we talk about it . . . ?"

or

"We think we have been more than fair in waiting for the $_____ you owe us. Are you being fair to us?"

or

"May we hear from you—soon?"

or even

"PLEASE . . ."

As was mentioned previously, your collection letters and notices should always go by first-class mail. In the later stages, to emphasize further the seriousness of the matter, it may be a good idea to use Certified Mail or even Registered—Return Receipt Requested. This mild measure of implicit intimidation may be effective with some people.

COLLECTION LETTERS AVOID CONFRONTATION

There is a curious paradox about collection letters. They take a great deal of your time and attention—and expense— to prepare them, to get them typed or printed, and to decide which letter to use for which customer and at which stage. And yet a collection letter or notice is just about the gentlest step you can take. That is because a letter does not *force* a response or reaction. It asks for one without insisting. It is very easy to avoid answering a letter.

By contrast, if you mention the unpaid bill to your customer in your store or on the street, or on the telephone, he cannot avoid responding in some way. This is a confrontation. No matter how he handles it—by evasions, excuses, promises, lies—a confrontation is an emotionally charged encounter that will almost certainly embarrass and probably also anger your customer.

Indeed, you may find that in some cases you will send one or even several collection notices and letters to a customer over a period of months, and during that same period you will have a number of conversations with him in which you both carefully avoid mentioning the unpaid bill. It takes five seconds to say something to his face, but in order to spare him the confrontation, which may lose him forever as a customer, you may decide to handle the matter by letter, which is much more expensive and time-consuming for you.

You will find, in fact, that many people become highly indignant if you mention an overdue balance to them (either in person or on the telephone) as your first collection effort. They consider this "dirty pool." They feel that you should send at least two or three notices or collection letters first before escalating the matter to a personal confrontation.

It is considered crude and impolite to talk about money, and of course it is also considered rude to bring up an unpleasant subject. The letter brings it up, but in a *noncontact* way, without forcing a confrontation.

Other Collection Methods

W E HAVE SEEN HOW SENDING A LETTER OR A SEQUENTIAL series of letters to your delinquent debtor is just about the gentlest step you can take; since a letter does not force a response, it does not produce an unpleasant encounter. Thus it spares your customer the embarrassment, even humiliation, of a confrontation in which he feels at a disadvantage.

CONFRONTATION

But sometimes you find that, even though your later letters become very firm and insistent, they do not produce results. Then you must escalate your collection efforts to the confrontation stage. After you have tried everything you could think of short of forcing the issue to confrontation, you must bring about a personal encounter, either face to face or over the telephone.

Either of these is a heavy weapon, although it may not seem so. Remember that you originally extended credit because you believed that the customer was an honest and responsible person, and you were probably right about that. But now time has passed, his account is overdue, and he has received and ignored a number of notices or letters from you. It is no longer possible to believe that there is a mistake or a misunderstanding, or that he doesn't know that he is overdue. He knows it very well, and since he is an honorable person he is very much embarrassed about it. It is this embarrassment that has prevented him from responding to your letters.

Now you will move to confrontation and force a response. Your approach to this encounter and the way in which you handle it should be guided by the same basic principles that govern all collection efforts. The central objective is to get your money as easily and painlessly as you can. The secondary objective is to do it without losing the customer, his good will, and his potential future business.

You should be friendly and flexible but firm. You should be polite but persistent. You should be sympathetic but skeptical of evasions, excuses, and promises. If you are angry, you must control your anger.

You have the edge in the confrontation in two respects. One is surprise, since the encounter will probably take place at a time chosen by you. The second is the moral advantage derived from the fact that he does indeed owe you money. Your moral advantage and his disadvantage produce embarrassment on his part.

As befits a polite person who has an advantage over an adversary, you should accompany your pressure and your insistence with a degree of graciousness. You are open-minded, you are reasonable. You are anxious to hear the reason for his failure to pay. (Up to a point, that is. You don't have to permit an endless recital of troubles and hard luck to be poured into your ear while message unit charges accumulate on *your* telephone bill.) You are understanding and flexible. For example, if it is not possible for the full amount to be paid at once, you are willing to discuss partial payment or setting up a schedule of payments.

Appeal to Sympathy

Even as you are extending sympathy to the debtor, you ask him to reciprocate. You tell him that your profit margins are not high enough to permit you to carry his obligation for many months. If you expected to do that you would have to raise your prices by a significant amount, and he wouldn't want you to do that, would he? You say that it is unpleasant for you to have to make this kind of call or request, just as it is unpleasant for him to hear it. He should spare you both this unpleasantness now and in the future by paying up on time.

Appeal to Sense of Justice

You appeal to his sense of fairness and justice. You point out that you showed faith and trust when you extended credit to him. He is being unfair to you: he is rewarding your trust by causing you trouble and costing you money. You are running a business, not a bank, and it isn't fair for him to use you as a bank. And while you are on that subject, you are paying your bank interest every day because you had to borrow what he owes you. If this goes on much longer you will have to charge him interest. You would not like to have to do that, but surely he can see the reasonableness of it.

Other customers who paid the same prices he did have already paid their bills, and it isn't really fair for him to get special treatment that others don't get.

Appeal to Pride

You appeal to his pride. You had thought of him as a prominent and prosperous citizen of the community, but if this sort of thing continues he will have a very different image. He has been known as a substantial and dependable person, but you are not finding him to be very dependable right now.

Threats

Thus, you appeal to his sympathy, to his sense of fairness and justice, and to his pride and vanity. These are the pleas, the appeals. Then you may have to move into another area and suggest that you will do things to hurt him. This is a drastic step. Now you are moving from *pleas* to *threats*. And threats are heavy weapons.

You should probably not use threats in the early stages of your sequential collection effort. As it advances you will hint at them and use them very subtly. Only in the later stages will you bring them out into the open.

You say that you would hate to see his image and his

reputation in the community damaged by failure to pay you. Then you go on to say that there is more at stake here than mere image. His credit standing could be affected. In fact, it definitely will be affected if this continues.

Depending on where you are in the dunning sequence, you may want to allude to other and more serious possibilities, such as contacting his employer, the further step of garnishment or bringing in a collection agency or filing a lawsuit. If you get to the point where you are threatening this kind of drastic action, it probably means that you have given up on him as a future customer and just want to get your money. It is pretty hard to maintain good will or a pleasant business relationship when such things as garnishment have been brought into the discussion. And you don't have to actually do it—just talking about it once is probably enough to destroy the relationship.

Making the Customer's Embarrassment Work for You

When you bring about this kind of confrontation, you are meeting someone who is at a disadvantage, someone who is backed into a corner. It is a corner that is made largely of his own embarrassment. Keep this in mind and try to find a way to make this embarrassment work in your favor.

For example, one of the most effective telephone techniques is this:

(1) Call the customer at home in the evening. This way you are more likely to get him on the phone immediately without having to deal with somebody else or leave a message. And he is likely to be more relaxed and less on his guard.

(2) Tell him briefly why you are calling and mention the amount he owes. But keep it short. Don't give him time to think about and prepare a response.

(3) Then pause—*and say nothing at all*—for at least ten seconds.

Unless your customer has nerves of steel (and few people do), he will fill that silence, probably with a rush of words that are impulsive and unprepared. And that is good for you, because you learn more from an improvised response than you do from a carefully guarded answer that is well prepared and rehearsed but also carefully contrived to conceal rather than reveal.

The same approach can work in a face-to-face conversation. In either case you must prepare yourself and prime your own nerves so that you don't break the embarrassing silence before he does.

The responses that you get in this confrontation conversation will fall into predictable patterns. Depending on the individual, they will be various combinations of denials, excuses, hard-luck stories, and promises—and outright lies.

The customer may say, "Gee, there must be some mixup somewhere, I'm pretty sure I paid that a couple of weeks ago." When you get this kind of vague response, there is a high probability that he did not pay it and knows very well that he did not. But you will not call him a liar or question his sincerity; that would serve only to irritate and would do nothing to speed the collection. Rather, you ask him politely but firmly if he will please take the trouble to look at his check stub and let you know the date and amount of his check. If he's "too busy to do that right now" or "I'll look later and if I don't find it I'll send you another check," then it is pretty clear that he never sent it the first time.

You have made your point, but don't stop there. You don't want to let him off the hook too easily. It is essential that you press for a particular date when you will receive the check. After the time and effort you have put into this, including a number of collection notices or letters, you will not settle for vague reassurances. You don't want to hear, "I'll get to it as soon as I can," or, "I'll take care of it."

Get a Definite Commitment

It is important to have an explicit understanding with him as to the exact day when he will put the check in the mail—the ideal, of course, is *today*. If he says, "I get paid Thursday, I'll send you the check Friday," your response might be, "Fine. That means we'll get it either in Saturday's or Monday's mail, so I'll make a note here to look for your check on Monday."

That makes it clear to him that, even if you allow an extra day for possible mail delays, you will be back on the phone to him Tuesday. Thus you leave him with a specific short deadline and the virtual assurance that you will be bothering him again immediately after that deadline.

This is the essential objective of any collection conversation—to make sure the bill is paid soon. It is not a friendly chitchat. You are not interested in good intentions or vague expectations. You want to drive that conversation toward a particular date, and you want to make sure he understands that you are making a note on your calendar.

The customer may say, "Oh, yes, I overlooked that. I'll send you a check right away." That is the answer you wanted, but his good intentions may last only until he hangs up the phone. Therefore, you don't thank him and change the subject to more pleasant things. Rather, you should say, "Good. Then I should have your check tomorrow or the day after at the latest." You reinforce his intentions by letting him know that you expect him to follow through.

Remember that the quality of your receivables deteriorates steadily as time passes. The longer he waits to pay, the less likely it is that he will pay at all. Therefore, it is essential that you have a definite and systematic and *scheduled* procedure of following up your overdue debtors. You must keep after them. You must contact them regularly and often until they pay.

It is important that the customer understands that you will persist, that you will not overlook or forget or forgive. A firm collections policy earns your customer's respect—not his affection, perhaps, but his respect. You want the customer to like you, but if it's a choice between liking you and paying you, the choice is obvious.

There is a certain type of individual who never pays his bills voluntarily or on time. He may have money in the bank and be perfectly able to pay, but because of a quirk of personality he never pays until pressed hard, until the payment is practically squeezed out of him. This is another reason for establishing a policy of regular, periodic, persistent collection efforts. This type of person will never pay until you press him hard. (When he finally does pay, you have a decision to make as to whether you want to keep him as a customer. Maybe he is more trouble than he is worth.)

First Confrontation Should Be Private

The confrontation conversation may take place in person or on the telephone. Whichever it is, you will handle it in the same way and say the same things. The first conversation should, of course, be completely private. You will add enormously to your customer's embarrassment and irritation if you dun him about a bill when he is in your store and other customers overhear the conversation. Similarly, if you call and leave a message with his wife or with a co-worker telling them the purpose of the call, you can expect a maximum of antagonism to result. To tell other people that he is a delinquent debtor is a very heavy weapon indeed. It should be used only in the late stages when you have tried all the gentle approaches without success.

Telephone Confrontation

Incidentally, when you are using the telephone you should be very sure that you have the right party before you deliver your message. For example, if you call your customer at home and ask for Mr. Jones, you might get his father or his uncle or his brother or his son. You may eventually reach the stage where you want to communicate with other members of his family, but you shouldn't do it by accident.

You probably should make your telephone calls to him at home rather than at work, at least in the early stages. This may be inconvenient and may require you or one of your employees to call in the evening. But he will be more relaxed and less on his guard in the evening at home. (He may also be drunk. Then he may speak more frankly and less guardedly, but it is also possible that he will not remember the conversation the next day.) Remember that you can get most working people at home between 7:30 and 8:30 A.M. And Saturday morning is another possibility.

Calling him at work is more threatening, because it raises the possibility that his colleagues or his boss may hear about it, either accidentally or because you intend to let them know. This is an appropriate technique, but it represents a massive escalation of pressure and should be done only when you are ready for it.

Occasionally you may want to send a telegram or mailgram. It costs more but it may be more effective than a letter in getting attention and in demonstrating your seriousness of purpose.

Surprisingly, collect phone calls sometimes work, too. Many people find it hard to refuse a collect call because they are afraid of being considered cheap. And if they do refuse it, they will know who it was from, and your message will register, anyway.

CUTTING OFF FURTHER CREDIT

One of your most difficult decisions will be whether to refuse additional credit to customers who are past due. Obviously there comes a point when you should do this. But these are judgmental decisions; each individual case is different, and there is no formula. You might lose a valued customer if you terminate his credit when he is ten days overdue and it turns out that he has been out of the country and hasn't seen his mail. On the other hand, if the present debt is uncollectible, it makes no sense to add to it.

TWELVE

Rough Stuff

Notifying the Customer's Employer / The Wage Assignment / Garnishment / The Sight Draft / Repossession / Skip Tracing / Collection Agencies / Lawyers / Small-Claims Court / Customer May Declare Bankruptcy

THERE COMES A TIME WHEN BIG GUNS HAVE TO BE BROUGHT in, perhaps from the outside. With a small number of your credit customers—let us hope it is a very small number—nothing you do seems to work. You have tried all the polite and gentle approaches. You have run through your complete stock of notices and letters. You have made or tried to make a number of phone calls. And you still haven't been paid.

(It won't make you feel any better, but you are not alone. In addition to tens of millions of overdue bills, something like one million unpaid bills are left behind *every month* by debtors who move without notifying their creditors, according to an estimate made by the American Collectors Association.)

Eventually you reach the point where the motivation and objective of your collection efforts change decisively. Now you forget about the secondary objective of keeping the customer's good will. You forget about the potential business that you once thought you might get from him in the future. In effect, you give up on him as a customer—he is just more trouble than he is worth. Now you just want your money. Once you get it you hope he goes away and you never have to see him or think about him again.

Up to this point you have tried to be gracious, you have tried to be considerate and to respect his privacy. You know that he is embarrassed, and you have purposely avoided trying to drive him into the corner or humiliate him completely. You have warned him that his reputation and his credit rating may be damaged, but you have probably not taken any active steps yourself to cause this damage.

Now you have reached the point where you abandon all politeness and restraints. Now you will do anything you have to—within reason and within the law, of course—to get the money that is rightfully yours.

NOTIFYING THE CUSTOMER'S EMPLOYER

One of the first strong steps you should consider is to notify his employer. This is easy for you to do; all it takes is one letter or phone call. But it is usually a very drastic step. Your customer's job is undoubtedly extremely important to him. And therefore he is very much concerned about his employer's opinion of him, not only his opinion of his work but his attitude toward him as a person. He wants his boss to think of him as steady and responsible.

Your message to the employer will severely damage your customer's standing in the eyes of his boss. The employer will understand that you have not taken this step lightly, that you have tried many other things before doing this. He will know that it is a serious matter. The employer will not be pleased to hear from you. He is trying to run a business or an organization, and he has neither the time nor the inclination to get involved with the personal problems of his employees. He wants them to do the job he is paying them for and otherwise not bother him.

In all probability he will call the employee in and say something like, "Look, I don't know what this is all about and I really don't want to know. Please just get your personal problems straightened out and don't bring them with you to the job. If you do it will affect your standing here and your future." That is all he will say, but that's plenty.

Calling the employer is strong stuff, but how effective it will be will vary according to how your customer makes his living. Generally speaking, it will be more effective with white-collar than with blue-collar people, and it hits harder in the higher salary and income ranges. It doesn't carry much weight in the case of a building-trades worker who is more concerned about his standing in his union than about his relationship with his employer.

One of the reasons that this step is powerful and effective with most employers is that it signals to them that even more trouble may be ahead. They know that you are telling them, in effect, that the notification is only the first step. The later steps will be difficult, time-consuming, and perhaps expensive for them.

THE WAGE ASSIGNMENT

One of the next steps may be a wage assignment. This has fallen into disuse in recent years and presents certain practical problems, but it is at least a theoretical possibility that you should know about. A wage assignment is an agreement between you and the debtor whereby you instruct his employer, with the debtor's consent, to send part of his wages to you. A wage assignment does not involve a court order or any court proceedings.

In years past it was a common practice to ask the debtor in advance, at the time the original credit arrangements were made, to give his consent to a wage assignment if that should be necessary. If this was part of your agreement when you extended credit, no further consent by the debtor is required. If not, it will be difficult to get his consent now. However, one way to do it is to tell him that if he doesn't agree to it, you will proceed immediately to garnishment.

A wage assignment is theoretically self-executing. That is, you send it to the employer and he does what he is told and sends you money. Well, maybe. And maybe not. Employers don't like to be put in the middle of a dispute that they were not involved it. They will feel that they should not be put to trouble and inconvenience, and possibly expense, to help solve a problem that is not theirs but yours. They will worry about liabilities and legal problems. They will also worry about the effect upon the morale of their employees—this employee in this case and others when word gets around. Finally, they may never have seen or heard of a wage assignment before. For any or all of these reasons, the employer may drag his feet, delay, deny that he received it, or flatly refuse to carry out the wage assignment.

GARNISHMENT

The next escalation step is the garnishment proceeding. Garnishment aims at the same objective as a wage assignment. It does *not* require the debtor's consent but it *does* require a court order. You go into court and prove that the debtor owes you money and that you have tried unsuccessfully to collect it, and the court then issues an order directing his employer to pay part of his wages or salary to you. There are limits set by both federal and state laws as to how much of his pay you can take; the reasoning here is that you have to leave him something to live on.

Every state has legal provisions and court procedures for garnishment.* However, the process has become more complex in recent years as a variety of restrictions have been imposed by legislation and by court precedents. Garnishment is a time-consuming, complicated, and expensive step, as all court proceedings are. And it has a devastating impact upon the debtor, psychologically and otherwise.

Many employers used to make garnishments grounds for immediate and automatic dismissal. This is now prohibited by a federal law, the Consumer Credit Protection Act of 1970. Still, there is no doubt that a garnishment proceeding makes a very unfavorable impression upon your customer's employer and is likely to severely damage his employment status and his career future.

It is also an unpleasant and expensive process for you. Be-

---

* In some states the garnishment laws provide that garnishment proceedings may not be used against a state employee, and federal law has long provided that you may not garnishee the wages of a federal employee or a member of the armed services. In an interesting sidelight, there has been litigation about employees of the postal service since it became a (theoretically) independent organization, separate from the federal government. At least one case has held that postal employees are no longer federal employees and are therefore subject to garnishment.

cause of the legal expense, it is not a very practical step unless the customer owes you several hundred dollars or more.

Garnishment proceedings are not confined to wages and salaries. You can garnish any assets of the customer's that you can find, such as, for example, a savings account or a deposit put down with another merchant on merchandise which has not yet been delivered. If the other party involved has a claim on the assets or the money, that claim takes precedence over yours. However, if he is simply a custodian of money that he is holding for your customer, your garnishment should force him to pay it to you. Of course, it is likely to be difficult to find assets which are not pledged or owed to somebody else.

THE SIGHT DRAFT

Another device you might try is a sight draft. This is a notice sent to your customer's bank directing them to pay money out of his account to you. (You can get the name of his bank from checks he has sent you previously, and you can probably also get it from the credit bureau.) A sight draft does not require a court order, but it does require the debtor's consent, and it also requires that he have money in his account. Considering the amount of trouble you are having with him at this point, it is likely that he has very little in his account and would not consent to your getting it, anyway. However, it is just possible that he might consent to it out of surprise and also to avoid even further embarrassment with his banker. It's a long shot, but it doesn't cost much and therefore might be worth a try.

REPOSSESSION

Sometimes you can try repossessing the goods you sold him. This is an appropriate procedure in the case of an automobile with considerable resale value, but it may not be too practical in other cases. You probably don't want to become the owner of used furniture, clothing, or small appliances, if you sold the customer those things.

There is a further question of who has title and whether you have the right to repossess. State laws vary, but your customer may be able to claim that he took title to the merchandise when you delivered it to him and that therefore you cannot repossess it. An exception would be an installment sale, if the installment contract provides that you retain title until the last payment is made, or if it specifies in another way that you have the right to repossess on default.

SKIP TRACING

Skip tracing is the term used in the credit business to describe searching for people who have moved away and left bills behind. You probably don't have time to become an expert in this special field, but there are certain easy steps you might take. Some people move suddenly with the definite purpose of trying to defraud creditors. Others move for other reasons but still leave unpaid bills behind. In either case they may assume that you will not take the trouble to pursue them. But you should.

Even if they leave no forwarding address, it is sometimes possible to track them down with just a little bit of amateur detective work. For example, the neighbors may have an address or know what part of the country they moved to. Or a neighbor might remember the name on the side of the moving van, and the moving company may help you. The post office may have a forwarding address. They are not supposed to give it out, but you may be able to find it out by sending a Registered Letter—Return Receipt Requested. That also has the advantage of letting the skip know that you have found him.

Friends or relatives may not be willing to tell you much, but they sometimes inadvertently give you clues. A former employer is a good source, because he may have been contacted by a new employer making a reference check. And if you have a written credit application with personal references, you should call them.

The new people who have moved into his house or apartment might know something—they may ge getting his mail. And similarly, the new people that now have his phone number might be getting calls for him and may have learned something from that.

This kind of sleuthing takes a lot of time and may or may not be worth it. You may decide, as many businessmen do, that once the debtor disappears it is time to write the debt off or turn it over to a collection agency.

COLLECTION AGENCIES

Collection agencies are specialists in collecting unpaid bills. They are usually private businesses operated for profit, although a number of credit bureaus that are co-ops also operate collection agencies. There are something like 5,000 or 6,000 collection agencies in the United States. You will find them listed in the yellow pages under that heading.

A collection agency will charge you a percentage of the amount they are successful in collecting, and normally they will charge nothing if they are unsuccessful. The charge might typically be 25 or 33⅓ percent. It may go as high as 50 percent on small accounts (say, under $50) or on those that are especially difficult, such as those for rent or those that are over twelve months past due. When the account gets up into higher three figures or into the thousands, a lower percentage is appropriate.

A collection agency will normally make a number of efforts to get your money for you. At some point they may decide it is hopeless and give up. In this case they should advise you that they have terminated their efforts, and then you are free to try another agency. And you probably should. The second one might be tougher or more diligent, or maybe just luckier, than the first.

Collection agencies are in a difficult business. Essentially they do pretty much the same things you have been trying to do. They use letters and phone calls and sometimes personal visits, although the latter are time-consuming and therefore expensive. They are probably more efficient than you are because they are more experienced than you and because they work full time at it. Some of them use rather vigorous methods which approach the strong-arm area. For example, they may impersonate police officers. They may make repeated middle of the night phone calls. They may threaten people with loss of jobs or even threaten physical harm. This sort of thing, in addition to being illegal, will rub off on you. People will assume that they are working under your supervision, and if word gets around this

could cost you a great deal of good will among all your customers and potential customers.

It is essential that you investigate a collection agency carefully before retaining them. They will not tell you if they use
improper methods. You should ask them for the names of several of their clients, businessmen like yourself, and you should
check these references carefully. Check the Better Business
Bureau, too. You should pay a personal visit to the offices of
the agency and have a look at the kind of people they have
working for them. You should arrange to listen to some of their
telephone calls and have a look at their collection letters. You
are also entitled to see their financial statement and their bond.
Keep in mind that they are collecting *your* money. They may
succeed in collecting from your customer, but if they are finan-
cially shaky you may have a second collection problem: trying
to collect from the collector.

In all probability the collection agency will insist that their
fee be paid on anything you collect from the time they enter the
picture. In other words, if the customer sends a check to you
two weeks later, they will claim their commission. Their argument is that he may have sent the check because of their phone
calls or other efforts. Many people will successfully resist all of
your requests, but they become intimidated when a collection
agency comes into the situation.

When you have a few accounts that are long overdue, should
you use a collection agency or should you just charge them off
to experience and forget them? This is a matter of judgment,
but there are at least two good arguments in favor of using
them. One is that, although their fees may seem high, you still
end up ahead of the game if they are successful. Suppose you
have a small account that you consider hopeless, and the agency
wants a 50 percent commission. If they collect it, you will get
50 percent. Fifty percent of something is better than 100 percent of nothing, which is what you will have if you don't use
them. And they don't charge anything if they fail.

Also, the money is rightfully yours. It is owed to you and
there is no reason why you should not use any proper and legal
means to try to collect it. Among other things, it lets all your
customers know that you take these things seriously and will

not overlook them. Your reputation in this respect is extremely important. If you think you have credit problems now, just let the word get around that you are a soft touch. Then you will have some *real* credit problems.

You probably should deal with a local collection agency, since you will be able to check on them more easily before you hire them as well as afterward. If some of your debtors have moved away and need to be pursued, the local collection agency will have reciprocal arrangements with other agencies in other parts of the country and can deal with them more effectively than you can. There will be only one commission charged, and the two agencies will divide it up.

Some collection agencies may offer to buy your accounts receivable at a discount. They will present the argument that you are sure of getting your money and that you won't have to spend any more time or trouble with them. However, most reputable collection agencies will not pay in advance, and those that do are likely to be a pretty rough bunch. Since they have laid out money to buy the account, they may go to almost any lengths to collect it. And your reputation will suffer for what they do.

LAWYERS

As an alternative to a collection agency, you may want to refer the matter to a lawyer. Some have a good deal of experience in this field, and some none at all, and you should check this. Many customers will be intimidated by a letter or other communication from a lawyer. Whether he says so or not, they assume that if he is in the picture, he is getting ready to file a suit. This may bring a check in right away, because many people are deathly afraid of being hauled into court.

Your lawyer is not likely to work on speculation the way a collection agency does. He will charge for his time, which means that if nothing is collected, you will have an additional out-of-pocket expense.

SMALL-CLAIMS COURT

One way to try to avoid large legal bills is to use the small-claims court, if there is one in your area. Normally you can file a simple form with the court and have the debtor brought in so that you can confront him. You don't have to be a lawyer or have a lawyer with you in small-claims court, and your debtor doesn't either. Proceedings tend to be brief and informal and generally unencumbered with legal technicalities.

There is no guarantee that you will win in small-claims court, though. Your customer might come in and admit that he hasn't paid but claim that the merchandise you sold him was shoddy or that you misrepresented it. If his story is convincing, you might get an unpleasant surprise, even though the law is on your side and you might win in a more formal court.

CUSTOMER MAY DECLARE BANKRUPTCY

There is one major hazard in lawsuits and indeed in all vigorous collection efforts. Since most of your collection problems are people who are unable to pay—because of bad luck, lost jobs, poor financial management, getting in over their heads, major illnesses—the debtor who is long overdue with you probably owes money to lots of other creditors, too. He hopes against hope that he will be able to work things out eventually. But if you or other creditors press him too hard, he may declare voluntary bankruptcy. More and more people are taking advantage of this procedure, and some have done it more than once.

Bankruptcy or reorganization proceedings are often very constructive in the case of a business that has receivables and fixed assets but a temporary cash problem. But when an individual files for bankruptcy he usually has some clothes, some used furniture, and a lot of debts. The creditors generally get little or nothing.

New Laws and
Other Recent Developments

Main Provisions of the New Laws / Abolition of the Holder-in-Due-Course Doctrine / Changes Due to Third-Party Credit Cards / Merchant Terminals / The Checkless Society—Will It Come?

THE PRACTICES AND PROCEDURES OF CREDIT HAVE BEEN changed in a number of important ways by a series of new federal laws that were adopted beginning in 1969. In Congressional debate and in discussion in the media these bills carried a variety of labels; among them, Truth in Lending Act, Fair Credit Reporting Act, Fair Credit Billing Act, and Equal Credit Opportunity Act. However, all of these were either part of or amendments to the Consumer Credit Protection Act of 1969, which was the first of the series.

Generally speaking these federal laws apply only to consumer credit, not to business credit. The laws and the regulations that implemented them impose a number of restrictions upon credit bureaus, credit investigators, banks, and finance companies, and indeed upon any business that extends credit to consumers or is involved in any way with consumer credit.

MAIN PROVISIONS OF THE NEW LAWS

Some of the more important provisions of these federal laws are the following:

- Finance or interest charges may not be included in the price of goods but must be stated separately in dollars and cents. Also, the customer must be told what interest rate is being charged, and it must be expressed as an annual rate of simple interest, not as a monthly rate, a discount rate, or anything else.

- If a businessman decides on the basis of a credit bureau report to refuse credit to a consumer, he must inform him of that fact and give him the name and address of the credit bureau. (However, you as a businessman are not required to tell him what the report said. In fact, your agreement with the credit bureau or agency very likely prohibits you from doing that.)
- If you as a businessman decide to refuse credit based upon information from some source other than a credit bureau or agency, you are required to inform the customer that he has a right to know the nature of the information, although you are not required to name the source. You may, if you choose, insist that he submit his request in writing.
- Whether or not a person has been refused credit, he has the right to demand that a credit bureau tell him whether it has a report on him in its files and the substance of the information contained in the report. If he has been refused credit, he is entitled to have this report read to him without charge. If he has not been refused credit or if he wants a copy, the credit bureau is permitted to charge him for it. The charge is usually less than $10.

  If a consumer asks, the credit bureau must tell him the name of everyone to whom they have sent the report in the past six years.

  If he disputes the accuracy or completeness of anything in the report, he cannot compel the credit bureau to change it, but he can prepare a statement of his own which gives his side of the story, and the bureau is required to add that to its report.
- If your customer questions the amount of the bill you sent him, you are required to acknowledge his question within 30 days and resolve it within 90 days. The law also specifies certain procedures that you must follow in discussing the matter with the customer and attempting to resolve it. Among these is a requirement that the customer be given

an opportunity to communicate with a human being rather than having to try to talk to a computer.

- If you retain a credit agency to prepare an investigative report on an individual (this is the more intensive report, which involves active investigation, rather than merely pulling out a file), you must notify the person being investigated.
- If a person loses his credit card and it is later used without his authorization, he is liable for the unauthorized use only up to $50. And if he follows the credit card company's prescribed procedures for notifying them of the loss, he isn't liable at all.
- It is now a *federal* offense to use a credit card fraudulently to steal goods or services with a total value of $5,000 or more.
- A credit bureau or credit reporting agency must delete from its report certain information, some of which could be considered quite important. For example, they may not report on a bankruptcy if it was adjudicated more than fourteen years before the report. And virtually all items of adverse information—including suits, judgments, tax liens, arrests, and convictions—must be deleted from the credit report if they are more than seven years old.
- You are not required to offer credit, but if you do offer it you may not refuse it on the ground of race, color, national origin, age, sex, or marital status.
- As was discussed in Chapter Seven, if you accept third-party credit cards or if you extend credit in any form, you are permitted to offer discounts for cash. No credit card company may deny you this privilege as a condition of doing business with them. A proposed regulation, not yet adopted at this writing, would provide that if you do offer discounts for cash you must post a notice to that effect and make the discount available to all your customers, not just favored ones.

Credit has become a very different ball game in the last seven years as a result of these new federal laws. Most of them carry criminal penalties for violations, and the laws are supposed to be enforced by the Federal Reserve Board or by other federal agencies. Some of them are probably going to prove to be difficult or impossible to enforce, but you as a businessman should not take too much comfort from that. Generally speaking, these laws also authorize civil suits for actual damages for violations and in some cases for punitive damages, too. Class actions may also be possible. Theoretically, you still have the right to use your best business judgment in extending or refusing credit. But there is no assurance that somebody won't sue you and claim that you discriminated against them illegally.

ABOLITION OF THE HOLDER-IN-DUE-COURSE DOCTRINE

Another major change that came out of Washington recently was the abolition of the "holder-in-due-course" doctrine. This involves the situation in which a merchant sells goods to a consumer on credit and then sells the consumer's installment note to a bank or finance company. The consumer then owes money to and makes his payments to the bank or finance company, which is called a holder in due course. That is, the bank or finance company is the legitimate holder of the debt, since they bought it for value in the due course of business.

Now, suppose the refrigerator breaks down or the car is a lemon and the buyer gets into a dispute with the merchant. He claims that the merchant cheated him or refuses to make good on his promises or his warranty. And the angry buyer refuses to make any more payments. The bank or finance company says, "We don't know anything about your car, that's between you and the dealer. Now you owe the money to us, and that isn't connected with your battle with him—so pay up." They were right and the debtor had to pay, under a principle of law that had been considered completely settled for at least 200 years. Even though the buyer might have a valid complaint, he could not assert this complaint against the third-party holder in due course (the bank or finance company) as a valid reason for refusing to make payments.

The first step to weaken the holder-in-due-course doctrine was taken in the Fair Credit Billing Act of 1974. This law provided that if a consumer finances a purchase on a credit card, any legitimate claim he has against the merchant may be grounds for his refusing to pay the credit card company or bank. Then, in May 1976, the doctrine was abolished completely by a ruling of the Federal Trade Commission. As things now stand, any complaint or defense the buyer has against the seller can also be asserted against any lender or creditor that bought his note from the seller. If you as a merchant are in the habit of selling your receivables to a bank or finance company, you will find that in the future they will be much more careful as a result of this new ruling, which overturned a settled business practice of long standing.

CHANGES DUE TO THIRD-PARTY CREDIT CARDS

In the years since World War II the whole credit landscape has been completely changed as a result of the introduction of third-party credit cards in 1950. Virtually all Americans in the upper economic brackets now carry one or more credit cards, and a high proportion of those in the middle brackets, too.

Many smaller merchants were pleased to turn over their credit problems and losses to a bank or a travel and entertainment credit card company. The larger and more prestigious merchants and department stores resisted the third-party credit cards at first, but many of them have now decided to accept credit cards as a supplement to their own charge accounts. And generally they now issue cards to their charge account holders, too.

If you accept third-party credit cards in your business, the acceptance may be routine and virtually automatic for smaller purchases, assuming that the signatures match and the customer doesn't look suspicious. If there is any uneasiness, or if the purchase is a large one, you will be required to get approval before accepting the card. You will have a printed list of cards that have been lost or stolen or revoked, but for large purchases you will have to call the credit card company while your customer waits.

MERCHANT TERMINALS

A relatively new procedure will make it possible for you to get immediate verification and approval for any and all credit card purchases. This can be done through the installation of a "merchant terminal" in your place of business. This is a small device (about the size of this book) that is connected over a leased telephone line to the bank or credit card company computer, which may be hundreds of miles away. You will insert the customer's credit card into the terminal and punch into the keyboard the amount of the proposed purchase, and you should get an okay within 30 seconds. These systems are complicated and expensive to install, so obviously they will catch on first in the major metropolitan areas. At this writing, American Express is offering merchant terminals to its participating business establishments at a charge of $50 per month.

THE CHECKLESS SOCIETY—WILL IT COME?

Now that they are putting merchant terminals in many stores and restaurants, the computer engineers and bankers have been doing a lot of thinking about another major change in consumer credit. This plan would speed things up not by approving credit faster, *but by eliminating it!* This is called EFTS—electronic funds transfer system. The idea here is that you would have a merchant terminal in your store that is connected through the computer and the clearinghouse to banks all over the country. You put the customer's card in the terminal, punch the amount of the purchase on the keyboard, and *voilà!*—the amount is instantly charged against the customer's checking account and credited to yours. No cash, no credit, no check. Just electronics.

According to its advocates, this electronic funds transfer system will inaugurate the checkless society, and this will happen very soon, perhaps within less than five years. Well, maybe. And maybe not. The banks would like it because it would eliminate the "float"—that is, the period of one to five days while they are waiting for checks deposited with them to clear the issuing bank. Another advantage to the banks is that the EFTS would dramatically reduce and eventually almost eliminate the billions of checks they now have to process with an army of clerks.

However, it is not at all certain that the public is ready, willing, or anxious for the checkless society. For one thing, many people are very uneasy about the idea of all kinds of people punching buttons and taking money out of their checking accounts. Second, many people are uneasy about computers, because they know that even the most advanced and most sophisticated data-processing equipment is operated by human beings, and mistakes are made. And they have learned from bitter experience that it is difficult or even impossible to get an error corrected after it is fed into the computer memory. Third, and perhaps most important, many people like the "float." In fact, they may like the float very much. They like the idea that you can put a check in the mail on Monday that will be delivered on Tuesday or Wednesday, will be deposited on Wednesday or Thursday, and won't clear their own bank until Friday or if they are lucky until Monday or Tuesday. Many people who cut things a little close manage to maintain an appearance of solvency only by virtue of the few days that it takes for checks to clear. They need the float in order to survive, and they will strenuously resist any efforts to eliminate it.

FOURTEEN

Summary and Conclusion

CREDIT, YOU SEE, ISN'T EASY. IT IS COMPLICATED, DIFFICULT, and time-consuming. And worrisome. And expensive.

It will give you problems, and headaches, and it will cost you money.

It involves risk and it will produce losses. If you don't watch it and control it very carefully, the losses can be large. It is even possible that if you are careless about credit and let it get out of hand, it can destroy your business and everything you have worked to build up. This has happened before, and it will happen again. It has happened to small businesses and to large ones, and it could happen to you.

Credit is based on trust, and its success depends on whether human beings keep their promises, whether they live up to their good intentions. And you don't have to be a psychologist to know that some of them won't.

If you extend credit to your customers, you will have losses. You will do everything possible to minimize them and keep them under control, but you will have them. That is perhaps one of the most important and most fundamental points about credit: there will be losses.

You will have a substantial amount of other expenses, too. In studying and analyzing the problem of credit, it is essential to make a realistic analysis of what these expenses are likely to amount to and to make sure that you include all of them. You will have out-of-pocket expenses such as membership in the credit bureau, the cost of credit reports, paying for employee time spent on credit, the discount paid to the credit card company or bank, the cost of collection letters, and the fees of collection agencies. These expenses are obvious. But don't overlook the other two expense items—both of them major ones.

The first is the cost of your money tied up in customer receivables. When you sell goods on credit instead of selling them for cash, you lose the use of that amount of money until it is paid. If your customers as a group owe you an average of $10,000 throughout the year, that is $10,000 that is committed to your credit program and that you cannot use for other purposes. You may have to borrow it, in which case you will have to pay interest. That interest is one of the expenses of your credit program. Or if you don't have to borrow it, you are passing up opportunities to use that money in other ways; thus, you are losing the potential interest or other earnings on that money. Either way, whether you borrow it or not, you lose interest or other earnings on that money.

The second major cost that many people overlook is the cost of your time and attention. As the manager of a business, you are pretty busy. In fact, you probably find that there aren't enough hours in the day. You frequently have to get by with less sleep than you need and to cut short the time you should be spending with your family. Therefore, your time is all spoken for, and there is a backlog of demands on it. Time spent on project A means that you will not get around to project J.

Credit involves management decisions that cannot safely be delegated to clerks or subordinates. It requires judgment, it takes a good deal of managerial time and thought. If you are in the credit business, you are also in the worrying business, and a good part of that worrying has to be done by you because it can't be done by anybody else.

One worry and one decision that you have to make yourself is the basic one: Is credit for you? There is no expert who can answer that for you. If you offer credit, you know that you will have losses and expenses. The size of these will be such that you will almost certainly have to increase your prices to cover them.

It is very unlikely that your profit margin on your cash business is so high that you can absorb all the extra expenses of credit. The question then becomes, Is it worth it? You hope that credit will bring you additional sales, but will it bring enough additional sales to more than cover the additional expenses? (And keep in mind that when you raise prices, you run the risk of *losing* sales.)

You hope that credit will induce your customers to buy more, to be less restrained and inhibited, to trade up to higher-priced and higher-profit margin items. You also hope that you will attract new and better customers that you don't have now, a wealthier and bigger-spending group. Will this happen? Will the additional sales to present customers and the new sales to new customers be enough to justify the expense and trouble?

There is nobody who can tell you the answer. Probably the only way to know for sure is to try granting credit and find out. The answer depends on many factors that are unique to your business and that cannot be precisely measured—the type of merchandise you handle, the type of customers you deal with, your location, your advertising, your image in the eyes of customers and the new image you might have if you succeed in changing it.

For example, some neighborhood businesses are more or less limited by the traffic patterns of neighborhood people. They patronize the business because they live or work in the neighborhood and it is convenient; rarely does anyone make a special trip from another area. Will credit help? Maybe, and maybe not. If this businessman thinks he is already getting practically all the business that is available from these neighborhood people, then credit probably won't add anything. In fact, it may be a negative if customers who previously paid cash now buy on credit. On the other hand, the businessman may feel that he is missing out on business that his customers are taking elsewhere where they can get credit. If this is the case, then there is a potential increase to try to capture, and maybe it makes sense to offer credit.

The basic decision on credit is a very important dollar-and-cents one, but no accountant can make it for you or even help you very much with it. This is because all the important numbers involve estimates and predictions with a wide margin for error. In fact, maybe estimates is too complimentary a word, maybe what they really are is *guesses.*

You know what your present pattern of business is, but you may not really know very much about your customers or how strong their loyalty to you may be. Or how they will respond to changes in your credit policies, which will include changes in your prices. For those to whom price is the only factor, or the major factor, in deciding where to buy, the change could be expensive for you.

It's hard enough to know for certain why people do what they do. It is practically impossible to know how they will respond to a different business approach. You can make educated guesses, or guesses that aren't so educated. You can follow your hunches or your business judgment. But there are no certainties.

Once you have made the basic decision and are offering credit, there are many aspects of the administration of the credit program that can be delegated. And now you have another decision, which is how much and how many of these details can be or should be turned over to specialists.

If you are operating a small business by yourself, or with a very few partners and employees, you have found that you have to try to be a Jack-of-all-trades. You can't hire an expert or a whole department of experts to do every job, as the big corporations do. You have to handle buying, pricing, advertising, hiring, dealing with regulatory agencies, trying to keep the burglars out, and so on. And so on.

Faced with a problem such as laying out your store, writing your advertising copy, picking your logo, and designing your signs and stationery, do you spend money to hire a specialist to do these things or do you try to do them yourself? Sometimes the consultant or the specialist will do a better job than you can do—sometimes, but not always. He will usually save you time, but maybe not as much as you thought, because you have to spend a lot of time getting him to understand what you want. He will definitely cost you money—no exceptions to that.

There is probably something to be said for the theory that the specialist will do a better job in his specialty because he spends full time at it. He has accumulated a lot of experience, he has made and learned from just about all the mistakes. On the other hand, even though he does a better job, it may not be enough better to justify what he costs. If you are building a large factory or shopping center, you will certainly need architects and plant-layout engineers and the like. But if you are going to open a small retail store or a printing shop with three employees, you can handle it yourself.

The same thing applies in credit. There are many areas of specialization and many parts of the credit and collection operation that you can turn over to a specialist. You either hire one or retain an outside consultant. Whether you do this will depend on your credit volume and how much the specialist will cost, and whether in your business judgment his special expertise is worth it.

For example, credit interviewing and the processing and review of credit applications is something that you can do yourself. Or if your credit volume justifies it, you may hire somebody to spend all or substantially all of his time on this.

Credit investigation and the checking of references is something that many bureaus and agencies specialize in. Their services are available to you at varying prices. On the other hand, much of this can be done by you or one of your employees, perhaps the same one who does the interviewing.

You will probably want to make the basic decision yourself as to whether to approve credit, and how much, for each individual customer. Once you have accumulated a batch of credit accounts, you can either tie up your own capital in carrying them or you may be able to factor them or sell them outright. If ownership of the accounts passes out of your hands, then the factor or lender will stand any losses and handle any collection problems.

The whole arduous collection process is one that can be handled by you or your employees or it can be turned over to collection agencies, who will do the same things as you can do. They are more experienced and probably more efficient at it, and sometimes just the fact that the agency has come into the picture is enough to produce results.

In addition to dealing with a number of specialists, there is another possibility. In many parts of the country the banks offer a service to retailers and other businessmen whereby the bank will take over and handle the entire credit operation from beginning to end. They will prepare and review the credit applications, conduct the investigation, make the decision, extend the credit, and absorb any losses. The customer may not ever find out that the bank is involved.

Some businessmen like the idea of turning the whole package of credit problems over to one specialist so that they can concentrate on other aspects of their businesses. It is hard to say whether this costs more in the long run. The bank's charges may be more or less than what it would cost to handle credit in house, including losses.

There is a certain sacrifice of flexibility under this program. Since the bank is taking all the risk, its decision has to be final as to each customer. The merchant might in some cases know a customer well and want to extend credit, even though the facts and figures on his application make him look like a poor risk to a stranger who does not know him. In such a case, the bank is likely to say, quite reasonably, "We'll go with this one on your say-so, if you really want us to, but you'll have to stand the losses."

Something like one million American merchants have decided to participate in one or more of the national credit card systems. While some of them use this as a supplement to their own credit or charge account programs, most of them are washing their hands of credit problems, so to speak, by letting the credit card people take all the responsibility. It is an approach that is worth serious consideration.

Our economy runs on credit and would come to a standstill without it. Credit is practically universal. Everybody does it, you might say. But the important thing for you is not what everybody does but what makes sense in your particular circumstances for your own business.

After all, when there are losses, they won't be everybody's. They'll be yours.

INDEX